# So, I woke up...
# Now what?

A new truth-seeker's self help guide on a spiritual journey to understand trauma recovery, the emotional body/your chakra system, uncovering the truth of human capabilities, and fully understanding energy flows.

### By Portia Dianne Lee

Copyright © 2019 by Day Seven Wellness
Published in the United States by WMS PRESS

Cover: WMS PRESS
Photographer: Author's Selfie
Illustrator: Lydia Ericson

All rights reserved. No part of this book may be reproduced, stored in a retrieval system, or transmitted by any means, electronic, mechanical, photocopying, recording, or otherwise be copied for public or private use (other than for "fair use" as brief quotations embodied in articles and reviews) without prior written permission from the copyright holder.

The author of this book does not prescribe financial advice or promote the use of any of the techniques as a method for financial, emotional, or medical problems without the advice of a physician, either directly or indirectly. The intent of the author is only to offer information of a general nature to help you in your quest for financial and spiritual growth. In the event you use any of the information in this book for yourself, the author, and the publisher assume no responsibility for your actions.

So I woke Up...Now What?:
A new truth-seeker's self help guide on a spiritual journey to understand trauma recovery, the emotional body/your chakra system, uncovering the truth of human capabilities, and fully understanding energy flows.

Published in the United States by WMS PRESS
ISBN # 978-1-7323425-7-6

For any ordering information or special discounts for bulk purchases, please contact us @ daysevenwellness@gmail.com

So I woke Up...Now What?:
A new truth-seeker's self help guide on a spiritual journey to understand trauma recovery, the emotional body/your chakra system, uncovering the truth of human capabilities, and fully understanding energy flows.

Copyright © 2019 All rights reserved. By Day Seven Wellness
1st Edition December 2019 Printed in the United States of America

# TABLE OF CONTENTS

Forward ................................................. vii
Readers Reviews ........................................... ix
Preface .................................................. xi
Dedication .............................................. xv
Section I .............................................. xvi
Chapter 1: Introduction To The Energy Body And Auric Field .... 1
Chapter 2: Social Psychology ............................ 27
Chapter 3: Introduction To The Tree Of Life ............. 39
Chapter 4: The Body's 7 Major Systems ................... 51
Chapter 5: Social Psychology ............................ 63
Section II .............................................. 78
Chapter 6: Personality Disorders ........................ 79
Chapter 7: The Manipura ................................. 95
Chapter 8: The Anahata ................................. 107
Chapter 9: Shambala .................................... 117
Chapter 10: The Anahata ................................ 129
Section III ............................................ 142
Chapter 11: Vishuddha .................................. 143
Chapter 12: Synchronicities And Social Psychology ...... 151
Chapter 13: Pyramids ................................... 155
Chapter 14: Tree Of Life ............................... 169
Chapter 15: Emotional Accountability ................... 179
Chapter 16: Conclusion ................................. 191
My Personal Invitation To You .......................... 196
About The Author ....................................... 198
Reference Page ......................................... 200

# FORWARD

**A**S WE RACE forward at breakneck speeds along this roller-coaster of life, there is a growing feeling among the masses that something in our collective reality is changing. Not just the kind of change that happens gradually in a progressive systemic way. Rather, this change is exponential. The very fabric of our reality is changing. At times it can feel out of control and chaotic. As if society itself is breaking down and the world is losing its grip.

The duality consciousness that has plagued us seems to continue to grow as we are continually being pushed by the mainstream into opposing camps. However, many are now waking up and recognizing something has been terribly amiss. There are choices to be made that need to be addressed by each individual and collectively as a society. No longer will the status quo be accepted. **We know as a collective that we can do better**. No, we must do better if the planet and society are not only to survive these changing times but actually thrive. These times call for true leadership. Not the ego-based greed centered leadership we have had. That kind of leadership has poisoned the planet and cost countless lives. These times call for wisdom. The kind that understands we are multidimensional spiritual beings having a human experience. **That there is a pressing need to heal ourselves, society, and the planet in a holistic way.**

We can and must develop a new society. A new way to live that is in harmony with all the beings on this planet. Portia Dianne Lee is a perfect example of the type of leadership that is so sorely needed. She is a shining light in the darkness that is guiding the way. She is ever learning, growing, and sharing with others her experiences and knowledge.

She understands the need to fully nourish the soul in a holistic manner. Taking the lessons of life and using them as rungs upon the ladder to higher consciousness. Truly this book is a blessing that is sorely needed at this time. Acquiring knowledge is unfortunately not enough. **Learning how to integrate it into our daily lives and continually evolve in EVERY expanding spiral of understanding, compassion, and love is what is needed.**

Portia Dianne Lee delivers that in this book. She understands the unity that lies behind all things. It is truly an honor to be a part of her circle and enjoy the light that she shines at this critical time in our own individual and collective evolution.

Together we can change this world and create a new Golden Age of Unity.

**Michael Stephen Lazaro**
**Evolutionary Energy Arts**
YouTube.com/Patreon.com

# READERS REVIEWS

Portia has given birth to a beautiful creation that will be a source of guidance and knowledge for all of us seekers. I could not stop reading... Portia's knowledge far exceeds the subject area of Social Psychology. Though one could argue that all areas relate back to the group as a whole. For example, Portia beautifully connects the psychopathology of cluster B... The Cluster Classifications are fairly new since the Diagnostic and Statistical Manual 5$^{th}$ addition and a bit better defined; Attachment Theory, developmental psychology; My favorite of all, synchronicity, Jungian analytical psychology (Carl Jung surrounded himself with a lot of smart women, their work as collaborative, he was clear about the feminine thought/energy for theory, history does not acknowledge) learning and memory and trauma... I'm going to be reading this book again and again!

**Dr. Jennifer Brown**
*ATR-BC, Psy.D*

I believe birth is sacred, however; the voyage from birth canal into this world by way of drawing our first breath of life is borne through a traumatic process. It is safe to say we all experience various degrees of trauma throughout a lifetime.

Through the guidance of Portia Lee's book documenting her own personal experiences I am learning how to recognize and deal with repressed issues- even in my own life.

I learned that recognizing physical/mental abuse affects the health of body, mind and spirit. Whether the abuse is from the bullies on the playground or the bullies in the boardroom. Having firsthand experience with bullies in the workplace I know the need for healing from their deeds; and I now know they too need healing.

Regarding toxic relationships in my quest to "eclipse people out of my life" her teachings not only acknowledge that it is okay to feel hurt, but she shows how to set personal boundaries in a healthy way.

Her phenomenal explanation of what and where the seven main chakras are in the body and their functions, how life's experiences can create blockages in one or more of the chakras leading to discomfort and dis-ease in the body. Portia shows how to unblock them through specific yoga poses, meditations and other healing modalities linked to each chakra.

Through spirituality Portia Lee divinely coaches you through awakening your conscious self, through learning how to unlock your spiritual gifts through the use of meditation, the science of yoga, use of crystals and how your angel guides communicate to you via synchronicities.

Portia Lee's book can show you how to experience joy in life. This work is keeping me on track, furthering my journey to the Whole me. I am positively certain that **"So I woke up…" will also ignite your light within, enabling you to see the light and energy in all that surrounds you as well."**

**Denise Leader**

*Yoga Instructor, Business Professional, and Intuitive*

# PREFACE

**D**URING THIS GREAT time of human existence, it is made overwhelmingly clear that there are many who are awakening to higher levels of consciousness and connecting the dots of the varying fragmentations we have been subjected to as a species and furthermore into varying cultures. As we each journey to seek truth and unified consciousness we are also led through a process of internal and emotional healing. It is rare that we as a species today are taught to care for our emotional bodies and to understand why and how to connect to each of our spiritual teams ascending humanity to a new level of consciousness.

As we witness such a pivotal time in our existence we recognize that there are many ways we can approach life and the conscious effort of most of us is gearing toward a community of conjunct human efforts becoming selfless in a time that our generations have been plagued with the encouragement to become internal and mutually grow from and within our traumas. Essentially, **this new truth-seeker's interactive self-help book connects the dots to the actual story of who we are as individuals based on the cyclical cycle of creation in an effort to ultimately end systemic abuse patterns of manipulation for its readers**. It is now that the generations are being called to uplift and support one another more than ever. If you ever ask yourself these questions, "how is this possible?" "why has this happened", or "who am I and why am I here?", through a refreshed understanding of our internal emotional bodies, then this book aims to respectfully answer those questions in one stop and at a comprehensive level.

I aim to bridge the gaps between emotional holistic consciousness, social aspects of psychology, spiritual concepts, and some of what we know through ever changing science from a basic perspective today and ultimately point out that we, as a woven fabric of varying cultures, are in fact more alike than we initially assume and have been taught we are. **The goal is help us collectively move our emotional body from a root level of consciousness and help us develop into the galactic beings as we are intended to be.** Living and operating from a heart space. **Knowledge without the work does not equate to evolution.** There are many of us today that have exceptional knowledge but still are tied hostage to a root level emotional existence and I, along with the guidance I've received, aim to help provide tools and resources within this book's contents to help us each individually ascend new heights and levels of understanding of one another and the communities to which we belong.

Throughout my journey to full awakening I have found many practices and techniques, so many that it is impossible to fully list them all here within this book. Coupled with my own internal "knowing", my spiritual gifts and abilities, and guidance have been enabled to put together a compilation of the rhythm of life and help further answer the why and how about our existence. There are a few interactive experiences within the book that I hope will enlighten each individual to their level of consciousness and the consciousness of all those they hold relationships with providing a deeper understanding and compassion.

The journey of writing this book has been such a blessing. I am what has been defined to me as a "Grand Master Practitioner" I hold several masters in varying eastern and aboriginal healing modalities. I am a person who has an affinity for everyone with a sincere giving nature, but especially those who are in pursuit of further understanding. I am eternally grateful that my journey has been ordered in the fashion that it has been executed so that the lessons aided by my efforts to redeem my spirit as a result of my traumas, share and provide these methods of fulfillment with my clients, and in turn share some of what I've learned with so many today.

I too once wondered "why me...?" in relation to my innate gifts and abilities and feeling that I had to hide them because of the conditioning of our society and I'm sure many of the readers of this work have at some point of their journey felt like that as well. **Keeping a conscious perspective of our lessons through our struggles is the actual work and once we are aware of the lessons the journey has unfolded, most wouldn't change a single experience and find a deep level of enlightenment.** Life can leave us bitter without the pursuit of understanding of what has happened when we've experienced trauma or a dark knight of the soul. I would like to help bridge the gaps on all accords and to open up each of those that read this body of work to a vast level of emotional peace. **We are meant to experience joy and peace in our lives.** Not strife, bitterness, and turmoil. Together, we are, can, and will continue to change global tides to unified consciousness.

# DEDICATION

This work is dedicated to my boys and the future generations to come of my bloodline and most of all, to all of my grandmothers... Edna, Irene, Dianne, Rose, and Mary helping us to clear our bloodlines of the generational curses of emotional trauma our bloodlines have sustained and passed down for generations like so many others have.

When you hear the origins of our stories... it makes sense. I'm so thankful to know. To my grandmothers, who now walk with me in spirit... Thank you for the answers. Thank you for being my guidance while here in the physical realm keeping my eyes open and for fully embracing all of my gifts, for allowing me to always be who I am, and for the encouragement they each gave me to move forward and take the steps necessary to heal. To my Nana, Dianne, my absolute best friend, thank you for the whole entire life of you... we will continue to have a blessed journey.

# SECTION I

**INTRODUCTION TO THE ENERGY BODY AND AURIC FIELD**
**UNDERSTANDING THE EMOTIONAL BODY**
**MULADHARA**
**ROOT CHAKRA TRAUMA**
**SOCIAL PSYCHOLOGY**
**HEALING RESOURCES**
**HERMETIC LAW**
**INTRODUCTION TO THE TREE OF LIFE**
**THE SEVEN MAJOR BODY SYSTEMS**
**SVADHISHTHANA**
**SACRAL CHAKRA TRAUMA**

CHAPTER ONE

# INTRODUCTION TO THE ENERGY BODY AND AURIC FIELD

THE TIME OF the divide and the veil of deception is now over, and the veil has been lifted. The times of indoctrinated religion that ensues the facets of our birth rights remain hidden and divided so that less than 1% can maintain power over the world are over.

**The times of the slave master mentality is being squelched within these seasons and it is time for a new level of consciousness to emerge among us all.** There are so many who are in search of the answers, confirmation, and communion their souls are yearning for revelation of, and this is an answer. Spirit has been guiding me to write a book for a very long time now. For years, I sat and thought to myself, "Which topic do I write about? What am I going to choose to say? Why me?" What message is the most important?" I've been involved in and seen so much. I've learned and applied so much…

The other thing that withheld me, was the fact that I, like so many of those of us who are awakened or awakening, was caught in surroundings of people who seemed to just not evolve. People who inadvertently stayed stuck in systemic cycles; exactly where they were within their individual traumas or chose to remain within judgement as they have been taught within indoctrinated laws.

After a bunch of misfortunes and a lot more triumphs, I wanted to know the truth about everyone I was around because of what I was seeing. The process forced me to take an internal perspective and take a lot of time for sincere self-reflection and to think of the people I may have personally done something unkind to, or lost my temper with or myself had been stuck in a cycle which as a result of my former projection/of my own internal pain and emotional blockages caused by trauma. **This is a journey about action, not only about attaining the knowledge.**

For clarification, I am not personally a "conspiracy theorist." We have an entire generation that needs us to heal. We owe it to ourselves, and we also REALLY owe it to them. Most of us want the best for our children. Let's kick this off by digging right into trauma. And you're here reading this to help aid your journey because you too woke up... or maybe this writing will help you to do so.

In order for us to understand where we are headed, not only do we have to know where we come from, but we have to understand how and why we feel what we feel. These writings are spiritual in nature as I am a deeply spiritual individual. They hold truth behind my testimony and how I've been enabled to heal so many.

For as long as I have been practicing healing work and energy work, my clients have always found me through a process of prayer. I never advertised myself as a healer or energy practitioner, yet and still so many have contacted me saying that they were suffering an ailment and they prayed about it and were advised or guided to contact me somehow. I've had hundreds of clients at this point, and the vast majority have come to me in this manner. Years ago, I had the honor to be shown my soul's divinity and my purpose. My personal purpose is to help heal trauma of all kinds and to do so in varying ways. I was chosen for this and it's what I'm here for. If you hold more of an agnostic or scientific point of view, please view these writings as the energy I will define which associates to the names and titles of the individual guides mentioned as it is all relevant and is tied to the soul/spiritual and scientific aspects that are being pointed out here.

Please keep an open mind because in these writings, I point out the links to all there is. This is not woo woo or new age… all that is written is absolute truth that has been withheld from the masses for so many reasons. On top of all that is written here, there is so much more! This is merely an introduction. **There is in fact no separation. Separation is an aspect of life we've been subjected to and unconsciously accepted and participate in as a result of our dogmatic beliefs.** Part of what held me back for such a long time was that I was trying to mitigate any backlash from judgement. Not fear, but the desire to not have to defend myself against those who were still asleep or stuck in their cycle. I no longer care and seeing the world in such a ravished state, I know, it's time to fully stand in my power to help in the aid to humanity and Spirit and help encourage in the way as I have been called to do. So, I woke up…

> "Don't let anyone have your integrity"
> – *Bishop TD Jakes.*

Simply put, Trauma is defined as a deeply distressing or disturbing experience physically and/or emotionally. Every single human being living today has been subjected to trauma and often times, there are many who don't even know it. Traumas are multilayered and consist of varying emotions and beliefs that become predictive patterns. There are several types of trauma. Each trauma we endure as individuals become stored within our emotional bodies manifesting themselves externally through loss, violence, physical injury and disease, and traumatic reactions resulting from threshold trauma. **Threshold trauma is the culmination of exasperating experiences over time**. It's "the straw that broke the camel's back" and is the most common.

When treating our traumas, it is crucial to understand the emotional body, and its energy channels allowing our understanding to help facilitate, release, and promote accessible reasoning which allows further comprehension of our emotional experiences/responses in the clients we serve. Your chakras *ARE* your emotional body! Our emotions are stored in the chakras, and our emotions can be used in our lives to help open us to the true beauty and wonder of the world, or they can create an internal prison or mask for ourselves later creating and manifesting themselves into physical disease and multilayered mental dysfunction.

**Untreated traumas, which again, we have all experienced trauma now, that manifest themselves into what is**

**called a phobic imprint (genetics through DNA and RNA) can and often times become a cyclical cycle that manifests continuously within an individual's blood line and emotional body causing impact to the individual's life experiences.** Phobic imprints can even be passed through generation to generation via etheric imprint. These phobias create energetic codes that send signals to both our energetic and physical bodies that the endured trauma will occur again and again should trauma not have the appropriate level of release which in turn creates blockages in our energetic channels, then to our mental processes, and lastly to our physical wellbeing.

Essentially the only way we can change for the better, is when we are willing to acknowledge, accept, and assume accountability for where and why we are where we are. Knowing what happens to your emotional body/chakras as a result of your experiences is key to understanding that. Prior to a change in mental or physical process trauma demonstrates its effect in and of us by showing the following patterns and identifying emotional and energetic symptoms:

- Overtangles
- Character Role Dynamics
- Secrecy
- Seductive Patterns
- Illness Seducing Entities
- Addiction Seducing Entities
- Fragmentations
- Blocked Memories
- Physical Injury
- Phobias
- Grudges

- Compulsion
- Conflict
- Lack of Boundaries
- Sabotage
- Self-Sabotage
- Personality Disorders
- Limiting Beliefs
- Curses
- Elementals
- Spirit Possessions
- Superimpositions
- Demonic Attacks
- Entities Attachments
- Negative Emotions

Throughout this book we will discuss each of the key identifiers above, the blockages each of these identifiers creates within our chakras emotional/energetic body, impacts of the blocked energy channel, and the varying techniques; resources; and spiritual guides to apply to your personal practice to help release these symptoms. Thus, holding space to allow us to be the best version of ourselves possible. We will also discuss the state of the world and how we have been programmed to become who we are and help shed light on how and a little bit of the why.

We've been led to believe that these things are "woo woo" or dark magic or that we aren't supposed to know. What you will discover here is the truth that we have been encouraged to stray so far away from so that our rightful individual powers would continue to be repressed; keeping us in a forever cycle of slavery. So, let's wake up....

## WHAT IS THE TRUTH ABOUT ASCENSION?

According to both Science and Aboriginal teachings, approximately 13,000 years ago, Human Consciousness was dispelled and placed under a veil/shield as the Bible describes as, "The fall of mankind." This was the fall of human consciousness descending us back in our evolution to where we are today as a collective humanity: Torn ideals and beliefs. Race and religion premised wars.

Destruction and mental disturbance are the norm and widely accepted and even encouraged. All, as a result of the destruction of unified consciousness. The unified consciousness of all living things is connected through a grid of electromagnetic fields that surround Earth within the ether for every single living species within earth. Every single one. In direct relation to human beings, there are three grids that help weave the fabric to human evolution. The unified consciousness grid is known for, fully documented, and controlled by most of the powerful governmental bodies, but the grid's existence and purpose are unknown by most people. The Unified Consciousness grid also comprises of these three energetic aspects:

1. Male energy
2. Female energy
3. Adolescent energy

**This Unified Consciousness grid is the energy that allows and holds a specific level of consciousness representing human's ability to reason and apply the aspects of the good-**

**and-evil/light-and-dark/feminine-and-male qualities that reside within us all**. This grid is directly connected to our individual emotional bodies through our chakras; it is the grid that connects each of us to one another, and to the Divine aspects of creation. As depicted in the book of Revelations, the Bible provides an interpretation of a parable for the end times prophecy widely known as the apocalypse. The reason for the fall is these grids have been formally shielded and manipulated from reach within the majority of human consciousness. Without full function of this Unity of Consciousness Grid, which is where we have been during this current era, humanity focuses primarily on the material world of the ego (3rd dimensional consciousness) and creates the possibility for our species to impart on major waves of self-destruction. Sound familiar? It should... we are living this way EVERY single day.

The largest energetic restoration of the Unified Consciousness Grid within our current times began by a few select and highly advanced Aboriginal souls around the planet (such as one of the greatest teachers in modern times, Drunvalo Melchizedek), with guidance started the repair of the grid... Thus, allowing us to awaken to our true purpose within this timeframe to in turn help rebuild and repair as many human spirits as possible, helping us ascend once again to a 5th dimensional level of understanding.

The awakening of the masses is coming. This is what ascension is and it is our turn to stand in readiness to help service humanity. In order to do this, we are destined to help each person we connect to, help restore their emotional body, by fully removing blocks first... beginning with our own. This has not occurred by mistake. If you are reading this book at this time, you are gaining in alignment with your higher self-consciousness/subconscious. You have been chosen to conduct the work you are here preparing for. Before your birth, you fully agreed to each part of this plan. In life… there are no mistakes.

## THE FLOWER OF LIFE

# THE EMOTIONAL BODY AND OUR CHAKRAS

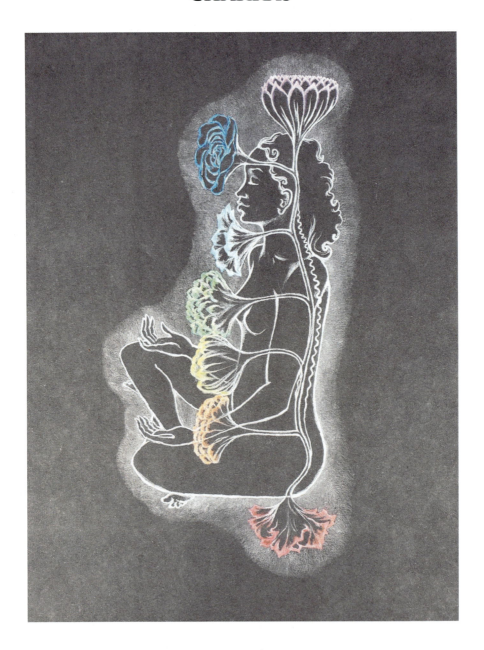

Every living species (over 8.7 million living species) has a basic design through and relating to the flower of life through the systematic repetitive pattern of its cellular structure. The unified consciousness grid we referenced surrounds the earth in layers that depict the flower of life.

Each living species has an emotional and energetic body comprised of frequency tied to the Unified Consciousness grid. Scientifically, each species begins with the Flower of Life molecular structure, but is further defined and categorized into organisms belonging to 6 major kingdoms:

- Prokaryote- Bacteria
- Protoctista- Aquatic and Amoeba
- Fungi- Mold related, Mushroom, Mold, etc.
- Plantae- utilize photosynthetic energy and are autotrophic trees and flowering plants
- Animalia- Two groups; Vertebrates and Invertebrates Birds, Humans, Horses, etc.
- Mineral- Crystals, Gems, and Stones (yes, they are living too!)

Our bodies are made of and from vibrational sound frequencies from Source, in the form of electric energy. I personally refer to this Source as, "God", "Heavenly Father, the creator of all things" or "Elohim", which means the creator of all things. What a beautiful source we have! Some refer to God as, "The Divine", "Source", "Allah", "The Universe", "Creator", "Science", "Father Sky"... etc., etc. It seems we are all more alike than we are led to or have chosen to believe we are! Our bodies connect with these electric currents and respond to the charge with frequencies that omit from our auric fields in response. Thus, participating in the process of creation.

As our Lord God of Hosts, Yeshua Ben Yosef one of my biggest personal guides in my work, also most commonly referred to as Jesus Christ, has been one of many known to famously recite, "As above. So below." This is actually what He was teaching as well as so many other Lords and scientists that many of us follow now. Each living soul also has an auric field, although each living species is somewhat unique in features. The electric currents we are able to perceive, and permit can be broken down into several initial categories.

Everything in this world is made of an initial sound comprised of a sound vibration which holds a frequency/vibration. Including our bodies and all solid objects. **Sound vibrations and the varying frequencies can be used to alter our emotional states and help us heal at a cellular level**. Most of what we are familiar with hearing and intaking in frequency is most of our radio/commercial music/even gospel music intake. They are typically recorded and played at a frequency of 174 hertz to 285 hertz which correlate to the root chakra/ego-based energy keeping us stuck at this level of vibration. **Our bodies have the ability to heal beyond these levels and can hear frequencies up to and proceeding sounds of 963 hz to help our cells heal and rejuvenate.**

Our auric bodies have seven components and can be referenced as The Seven Bodies of Man. As we clear through life's vast traumas, which is what we are all here for, we activate the vibrations within our auric fields as well. These are the energies that precede us in being and the energies that make us attract our environments. Our associates usually maintain the same energies that we omit within our auric fields that's why the saying, "You attract what you are" is not always accurate. Darkness is often attracted to light because the light is darkness's attempt to fill its void... This energy system is actually still to current day much of a mystery among energy practitioners and intellectuals alike. The seven bodies that our auroras consist of are:

1. Physical Body- connected to our emotional body's chakra, the Muladhara which is also known as the root chakra which is connected to our sense of safety.
2. Mental Body- connected to our Svadhisthana, the Sacral Chakra sexuality and sensuality.
3. Astral Body- connects the Manipura, Solar Plexus willpower and confidence. Connects to the electric currents of the universe and spirit which connects us to all that is. Soul.
4. Etheric Body- Anahata, connects the Heart chakra. Unconditional love, self-love, and love for all that is.
5. Power Center Etheric Body (A center of power)- connects the Vishuddha- Throat chakra. Creativity, self-expression, and truth.
6. Spiritual Body- connects the Ajna, which translates to the third eye and our epiphysis cerebri which is our pineal gland.
7. Line of Wisdom Ketheric Body connects to the Sahasrara, our crown chakra. This is the connection

to the Goddess, the divine. Mother Earth. **This channel actually is only fully activated when all energy channels are clear and grounds itself from our root through each of our chakras creating a source of energy that omits from us in the same form as a lotus flower.**

We will discuss our seven auric fields and seven basic chakras more in depth as we touch on each chapter's in detail.

Sharing as background knowledge... The energy currents we receive can be categorized as follows:

- Spiritual
- Mental
- Astral
- Etheric
- X-Ray
- Light and Color
- Heat
- Electricity
- Sound
- Solid

The specific details of each of the above frequencies are a master and grand master level subject knowledge. We each start our journey's as beginners in the help seeking phase, to practitioner, to expert, then master, and grandmaster, etc. Each of these phases in our journeys hold great respect and accountability within each. Please allow yourself time to become familiar as a practitioner of the emotional body wellness **before** delving into these topics. For the outline of this understanding, I will provide a brief explanation as it relates to universal laws called "Hermetic Principles." Having a general knowledge of these principles is a great base that can provide compounding knowledge with experience for years to come.

So... Let's take our time. The mastery to this insight and knowledge is true soul mastery and comes forth when all energy channels are clear. Practice, practice, practice and then, practice again until you sincerely make a change on an internal level. **Everything about your life and the way you relate to the world will change with practice.** Experiencing each level of ability unfold for ourselves as lightworkers and then within our clients; that is one of the most amazing blessings this journey has to offer.

## "MULADHARA" ROOT CHAKRA SYMBOL

The root chakra is at the base of our spine, correlates with the color spectrum and frequency of the color red. The sound correlation for this frequency is 174 HZ, 285 HZ, and 396 HZ. This chakra has 3 additional energy currents which happen to be as powerful in their own respect as a fully functioning chakra. The four energy ports and channels that make up the root chakra are:

- The Muladhara (Root Chakra)
- Left Axillary (Meridian Channel)
- Right Axillary (Meridian Channel)
- And the soul Star

The Muladhara, the root chakra dictates and controls our gender and is the basis for our sense of safety. This is the home of the energy tied to sexuality and sensuality. Yes, sexuality and sensuality are two different energies! Masculine energy holds the aspect to the emotion tied to sexual energy and the Feminine energy holds the emotion tied to sensuality and are each tied to the left auxiliary and right auxiliary. In current times, science and metaphysics have each identified that the masculine and feminine energies don't actually correlate to gender specification. It is believed that the male and female sexual organs do not always match the energy tied to the soul's emotional body. This is one of the many reasons why we will not delve further about the subject in these chapters. Neutrality is a great standpoint for this topic and all topics that we are not meant to understand as we cannot adequately dictate the lessons and opportunities on an individual soul journey.

The Kybalion, Hermetic Principles and Philosophy is a work published and translated by the "Three Initiates" is the teachings of ancient Hermeticism defining the laws of life's existence. This work defines how the law of attraction is possible and why. It is derived from the works and teachings of the Greek God Hermes who is perceived as a reincarnated soul of Egyptian God Thoth and Mayan God Quetzalcoatl. Thoth, Lord God of Divine Worlds/Hermes is also believed to have been a guide of Jesus and helped to influence his teachings.

Billy Carson (who I follow and who's work I adore) is a research scientist, metaphysics, and more recently, released a book in honor of Thoth/Hermes and his work and teachings called "The Compendium of the Emerald Tablets." I strongly suggest this read, but for this work I have been guided to reveal the aspects of trauma on the emotional body and correlate them to the teachings of the Hermetic Laws and Principals. Taking a bit of a deeper dive… It is also believed that Thoth is accredited to supplying us with additional DNA strands, similar to what is happening now, so that we could live out more of our human capabilities and tap into our inner truths. Thoth is also one of my personal guides.

The Hermetic law that correlates to the Muladhara/root chakra is the principal of gender. This law recites: "Gender manifests itself on all planes as the feminine and masculine principles…. The masculine principle is always in the direction of giving or expressing, and contents itself with the "Will" in its varied phases. It is said that there must be balance in these two forces."

Trauma is more specifically tied to our physical body aura and root chakra energy. Often times, humanity does not have the ability to fully function within the higher-level chakras and will occasionally vacillate between the use of them.

## SOUND FREQUENCY

Because our universe is made entirely out of positive and negative vibrations, (electrons and neurons; masculine positive electric and feminine negative magnetic) each sound within existence holds a vibration that has an effect on the emotions, mind, and body of living things. Music is used to enhance a meditative state, relieve pain, facilitate miracles, enhance awareness, and more. Solfeggio music works in direct correlation to our chakras. 174 HZ is the sound frequency that holds a vibration that helps cure the auric field around you. It is the introduction to internal stillness which allows us to enter a state of awareness. 174 HZ helps us relieve physical pain and helps us ground through our Muladhara. I really prefer the work of "Meditative Mind" which can be found via YouTube and iTunes and other resources. So far, they have one of the most comprehensive listing of sound frequency libraries that I've seen that correctly help heal and aid clearing of our chakras and emotional body.

## FOOD AND BEVERAGE TIES

There are many reasons why trauma ties directly to food. Foods we make choices to eat to self sooth, foods we are introduced to as a means of nutrition, fallouts of poverty and government funded and supplied food, and lack of knowledge or resources. Newly trending food chain discrepancies among the racial divides as well as some races can tolerate foods that others cannot... That's a whole 'nother subject!! To list a few and keep the subject brief (after all, I am not a nutritionist) but food can and is in fact directly linked back to the emotional wellbeing of each of our lives. Much of the food atrocities this generation faces are not hidden and with waves of people airing toward veganism larger than ever seen before in recent centuries. Food is directly tied to the following fall outs of trauma for example:

- Cancer
- Autism
- Mental Health Disorders
- Diabetes/ Blood Sugar Disorders
- Obesity
- Digestive System Disorders
- Anger/ Aggression
- Self Esteem
- Etc.

To aid in our physical and emotional healing a proper diet pertaining to us as individuals and according to our blood types is key. **But before you do anything... if you want a healthy mind, listen to your body!** Pay close attention to the way your body responds to what you are feeding it; no matter what you've read or heard because you could tolerate an intake that others cannot or vice versa. **The cleanest way to eat and has been proven is vegan** (*I am not a vegan but am extraordinarily health conscious and aware of what I can and cannot tolerate in order to stay emotionally and physically balanced*) and veganism also ties to our mental and emotional wellbeing...**Routine fasting and digestive track flushing can also help promote emotional**

**wellbeing and trauma recovery when done regularly.** I'd highly recommend that each individual consult with a health coach or nutritionist to see what diet best suits you. And again, make sure to know your blood type.

Because the Muladhara correlates to the red color spectrum natural foods and beverages deriving from the red and brown spectrum provide the most healing qualities to our root chakra. Helpful hint, when I plan out Day Seven's trauma relief sessions, I always incorporate food. With my intentional selection, I am helping each individual have the utmost benefit for their healing experience within my setting. The Muladhara is our nurturing center and can help us indicate where we as individuals are, energetically speaking, and gives us a base to understand the focus of what our emotional bodies are communicating to us through our food cravings.

Food cravings tied to the root chakra are typically soul foods, hearty meals, chocolates, protein rich, peanut butter and other savory pallets. Because much of our western culture operates within the root level, this is one reason why we see such an abundance of obesity. When preparing a healing spread for a group with a focus on a healing subject matter related to the root chakra, you can enhance the healing experience with these types of items: beverages and teas should correlate as well. Darker colored herbal blends help most with quick energy flows. I offer and encourage each of my clients to sip tea while we work together to help while I conduct focused and targeted energy healing. Aside from the medicinal qualities within herbal blends, all teas contain functioning heart health aids.

Generally speaking, when our Muladhara is functioning freely, we have a full understanding of our foundation of life. Our basic needs of survival are located within it and are the basis of our relationships in addition to how we relate to them. The energies of Mother Goddess, Earth, Gaia, omit magnetic and negative charges of energy currents to these energy portals. The negative charge can be further understood because the dominant feminine feature is a receiving energy. This is a station for stability. Empowerment. **When we have a healthy Muladhara, we have healthy active digestive systems, balanced responses to adversities, and can stay grounded in healthy relationships.** Our unified consciousness is connected when we are both activated and balanced and flowing in our root and crown concurrently within each functioning chakra in between.

Our Muladhara is tied to the realm/aura of our physical body as well as our actual 'physical body." From a hidden ancient knowledge, a Hermetic principle explanation, the Muladhara correlates to the principal of gender. "Gender is in everything; everything has its masculine and feminine principles. Gender manifests on all planes of correspondence. This principle embodies the truth that there is gender in everything." Our physical body is also connected to the element of earth. The importance of our connection to earth within the functioning of this chakra provides many positive results. I will list the following:

1. Active intuition
2. Healthy Relationships/Unified Consciousness
3. Removal of root level entities
4. Promotion and support of survival of all things
5. Productive and selfless ego.

The list can be vast, but for the focus of this curriculum we will air on the general and most common behavioral traits of root level trauma. An underdeveloped or blocked Muladhara can be enticed by one of the following **life occurrences or personal relative emotion which is categorized as "ego"**:

- Sexual Trauma
  - Lack of boundaries, sexual abuse, rape, gender programming
- Self-Centered Ego
  - Selfishness, Narcissism,
- Digestion Disease (including diabetes)
- Fertility
- Addiction
- Anger
- An individual who creates or is the facilitator of unhealthy relationship patterns
- Unhealthy Maternal Relationships
- Etc.

Most of the energy tied to the Muladhara is tied to the energy that omits from the ego. Our ego self is our personality and begins forming in utero. All internal beliefs which make up our ego are initially formed within our utero experience and then first connect our feminine aspects of life. No matter our gender, we first connect to the feminine aspect of our personality. **The feminine aspects of our personality are governed by our "unconscious self." These aspects are tied to the teachings we received or lack thereof on the contrary. They dictate our desires and yearnings based on the health of our maternal relations.**

Generally, the right side of the body governs masculine energy and the left side governs feminine energy just as the sun has similar qualities and drives and motivates masculinity and the moon influences the femininity.

The ego holds our connection to the material world, guidance throughout our soul mission, and our unconscious self. It is very typical that we will service clients who are unknowingly stuck with the root cycle. Most of humanity currently exist within the functions of the lower three chakras.

When we are flowing freely in our Muladhara, we have a better chance at connecting to our higher selves. As lightworkers, it is our job - done at best - to help each person we influence to connect to the highest level of consciousness within each client's experience with us as an earthly guide.

**Unresolved trauma or wounding to this area is the most rapid transition to low vibrational frequency and blockages of our emotional body as it holds the least amount of space within the energy field. Each human being has an imprint of this transitional energy.**

## SPIRITUAL GIFTS

The spiritual gift that is tied to our Muladhara, root chakra, is the gift of intuition. Intuition is the ability to understand a concept immediately, an internal knowing that does not require conscious reasoning. Our intuition is housed by our 3rd brain, which is connected to our root chakra region, our intestinal system. Intuition ties to instinct. Instincts project themselves into our reality by proving our unconscious thought patterns with a response to our environment and relationships based on our internal perceptions.

**A healthy and functioning intuitive ability allows us to work through life on the basis of trust and unity allowing these energies to flow and transmit to our environments healthily.** Blockages within the root chakra ground our intuitive abilities to internal knowing. They create self-inflicted outward identifiers. False intuitive feelings about the world and relationships around them. **Self-sabotage is the most common result of an inward projection and misuse of our gift of intuition. We become guarded to the inner knowings and for varying reasons, primarily for fear of judgement in our modern-day belief systems and begin to lose confidence in our intuitive knowings which in turn reduces our connection to nature and disconnecting from Mother Nature's natural healing ability.**

## CLAIREMPATHY

Clairempathy, (not to be confused with empathic abilities which is actually clairsentience) is a gift that enables to sense or appropriately identify another's emotions, thoughts, or circumstances. Clairempathy is an internal gift we are each born with and is the most common gift among our species. A healthy root chakra fully supports a fully functioning gift of clairempathy. This gift can come and go throughout our lives based on our experiences and when we are in a state of flowing Muladhara energy. With each of our spiritual gifts, it is important (especially for lightworkers) to manage our nature so that we do not experience overload.

Skilled practitioners maintain spiritual boundaries identifying when it is appropriate to use and apply their gifts without being invasive or breaking boundaries of our counterparts. Essentially, it is not ok to use any spiritual gift for self-seeking, self-gratification, or manipulation. It is also crucial that as practitioners of light that we appropriately apply radical self-care, maintain spiritual boundaries, replenish our energy, and clear any unwanted or uninvited projected energy from our auric field and the utmost protection.

The difference between clairempathy and clairsentience is that empaths "sense" emotions and sentients actually emotionally and/or physically feel the experience of others. Empaths sense the energy; sentients feel the energy.

CHAPTER TWO

# SOCIAL PSYCHOLOGY

**SOCIAL PSYCHOLOGY IS the psychological response to our experiences in the form of actions, thoughts, and feelings.** We will touch briefly on the societal aspects of each theory our emotional systems are tied to by the governing energy body to further understand how each energy body processes our internal communication and drives an impact to our internal mental processes.

Within the knowledge of social psychology there are several theories when further examined that can be further applied to understanding how trauma to our energy bodies is stored and then manifests in relation to our world dictating our interpersonal and personal relationships. Aristotle and Plato are two of the most famous social psychologists.

*"Be kind, for everyone you meet is fighting a harder battle"*
*– Plato*

**THEORIES RELATING TO SOCIAL PSYCHOLOGY AND THE ROOT CHAKRA ARE:**

1. Self-Perception Theory- when an individual fully believes a lie. Individuals shape an understanding or feeling about a situation or an action. This

is an individual who sees themselves in the same way that they see another. Right and wrong then becomes based on whether or not they personally would enact the same way that a response or action was given by another.
2. Social Exchange Theory- Rationalization of how an individual can benefit or gain from another. Individuals can instinctively apply a cost benefit formula to identify whether or not a relationship is worthwhile.
3. Social Verification Theory- A person's need to be accepted. How they perceive themselves is how they want others to perceive them.

Take a moment to identify if you or anyone you know applies to these theories. Chances are if these qualities are identifiable as clearings that can be done to help release stored energy and bring balance to an overarching thought process.

Take a moment to document any key phrases, catch statements or actions we may identify when consulting our ourselves, family, friends, or clients that would directly correlate to root chakra blockages.

| Key Phrases | Catch Statements | Actions |
|---|---|---|
|  |  |  |
|  |  |  |
|  |  |  |
|  |  |  |

## **IDENTIFYING ROOTS**

Root magic is tied to the practices of Hoodoo and Voodoo. Offering my personal opinion before I introduce the subject matter I've selected to share around this knowledge, I do not personally believe we have a right to interfere or with manipulating the will, ego, or decision making of any other living being. For the principals related to trauma that we will review as a result of trauma response, I will continue on an unbiased stance as to the spiritual practices tied to both of these subjects, but I do need to make my personal belief known in relation to practices that may promote, enslave, and create bondage of an individual's will of any sort. Much like the bondage we all have been placed under for such a long time at this point in human existence.

Why is it important to understand this aspect of the emotional experience? The vast majority of us are or have been under spiritual attack in which we seek assistance for and from. Most of us go to mental health practitioners, pastors, doctors, friends, and family members to hold space for us during life's challenges and adversities. Especially true of our western culture and belief structure, we have been encouraged to be blinded to what is real. Being from a culture that has a drive toward enslavement through manipulation, we have been misled and extraordinarily miseducated about the full capacity of our existence and our soul's purpose. On the contrary, with the way that things exist today as they have for generations passed, we have descended and reversed to a very low level of consciousness. We will discuss consciousness and its many layers in a later chapter. But we have more ability than we are "allowed" to publicly acknowledge. Understanding the emotional body down to the science helps us understand the real and full functioning capacity within the human soul.

This is not a game. A root can be transmitted to another being through ritual practice by placing the other under a tie/root to their unconscious state of mind and can actually supersede generation to generation. These ties/roots are driven by and individual's own emotions: fear, lust, and addiction which are aspects of our unconscious ego self to further be driven by the belief system they were influenced to believe in utero onward. It is important for us to be able to identify the occurrences of our clients, family, and peers as they may come to us for help and when we can adequately assess their emotional blockage, we can help to set their soul free from the bondage most of us do not choose. **Freeing ourselves from unconscious thought is the most promising gift we can receive within the realm of human consciousness, but it is the hardest of all works to do and takes MANY years.** Look for the signs listed previously to identify the symptoms tied to root chakra dysfunctions and signs of root related magic.

## CONNECTION TO MOTHER EARTH, TRAUMA, AND ROOT MAGIC RELEASE

Nature is not the sole cure for all things, but it can provide an answer for everything as everything in our physical world is derived from it. Root level blockages can be largely cured and removed by simple engagement. The earth has made a commitment to each of us in its own living consciousness just as we have a commitment to it. Nature can connect to us through each of our energy sources. And to allow the earth to work its own healing abilities we must connect with our physical bodies. Because our first connection to life is one of nurturing feminine relations, the earth does just this in question to each level of stability. **Just like each of us, mother nature holds a healing energy and will and does help us heal just as we are to reciprocate.**

Eight years ago, I began to practice stoicism through the teachings of Tao which hold virtues of self-control, tolerance, integrity, and virtue. **Stoicism is the practice of main-**

taining emotional control. This is the pendulum swing of life. **The idea is not to swing too hard in one direction because you will inherently swing hard in the opposite direction.** All emotional experience and expression live on the same scale of polar opposites. For example, love is a polarity of hate. **You can't hate something you never held love for.** The goal here is balance. Nelson Mandela (one of my most esteemed heroes since childhood), Seneca, and Socrates were all in some ways stoics and also practiced stoicism Tao principles. These practices can be tied intimately to Buddhism, Chi Gong, Tai Chi, as well as Tao and are a fundamental path to humanity. **The idea here is that self-control is what leads us to a better and justified humanity.**

Nature and our connection to it and everything of it, helps to cure a multitude of emotional imbalances. Just sitting with a tree; I am aware that some people would consider that tree hugging, (and I'm okay with that) will bring forth the deepest level of peace and centeredness. These activities have bought me, my clients, and my many students throughout the year's peace and fortitude. It's really time for us to get connected again.

## HOMEWORK ASSIGNMENT

Find a safe and quiet space outdoors where you can sit in meditation with the earth for the next 7-days.

Choose a spot that is grass filled, dirt filled, or a stone. Spend 10-minute to one hour in this location. Ask Mother Earth to remove any blockage or pain within your Muladhara.

To start, place your hands stably at your sides palms down and connected to the earth as you sit, or lay. Preferably with headphones, listen to a solfeggio beat of 174 HZ for the first few days and gradually increase to 396HZ.

Each day incorporate just one yoga asana to end your meditation. These can be googled and researched for the root level to increase your vibration.

Keep a journal to document changes in your experience or any insight you may receive during or after this meditation.

It is also a great idea to review the TED talk of the great game changer Dr. Nadine Burke Harris which can be found on YouTube. If you have additional time, please watch or re-watch the movie "Interstellar" featuring Matthew McConaughey.

## PERSONAL TESTIMONY:

*Trauma and blockages shut down energy flow in our emotional bodies creating vast side effects up to and including death and shorter life spans. Kundalini is a burst of energy that increases the frequency emitted by an individual. As a trendy fad, there are a lot of promotion of ways to raise the kundalini, which typically work, even though not all are safe, but only when you have clear flowing energy through your emotional body. You can't fight it when kundalini moves through your body. It is most commonly described by church goers as receiving the Holy Spirit and usually a milder exposure to the experience.*

*In short, I have dedicated many years of my life with a focus on inner child healing as a result of the extreme dys-*

functions I was raised with. In my childhood I had experienced systemic cycles of neglect, child molestation, physical/mental/emotional abuse, I was snatched by a stranger and subjected to unhealthy relationships with individuals who had untreated and unmanaged mental illnesses. Again, not at anyone's fault per se, just being stuck in a cycle that so many are not aware of because you don't know what you don't know until you do. Prior to this journey, I had several diagnoses that for my then uneducated mind, needed healing of my root chakra and emotional body.

Although I had the experiences, I can't knock them, and I wouldn't trade any of them. Everything happens for a reason and the type of knowledge I gained has enabled me to help and honor so many others.

Diseases I suffered from began with chronic constipation, endometriosis, gastroenteritis, chronic diarrhea, 2 calcified tumors, one in my breast and colonic benign tumor and lastly 10 malignant colon polyps. Malignant is dangerous, but they caught the polyps early enough that the cells did not mutate or metastasize. About 50% of most people over 50- years old who have the unfortunate diagnosis of a colon polyp have 1 or 2. I had 10 and 2 tumors.

**Based on my own research, I found that cancer is actually a group of diseases that compound to create abnormal cell growth.** I was advised that due to the severity of the diagnosis at my then very young age, I had to have a colonoscopy (which are noooooo fun) once a year for the rest of my life. I immediately had the intuitive knowing that I had to dedicate myself to a journey of inner child healing.

*In my case, my fully functioning intuitive knowing kicked in a moment of surrender, turned from an internal process of intuitive knowing to a collective conscious perspective. I went through vast cycles and techniques of emotional healing, changed my diet, and began furthering my education around the emotional body and trauma recovery. I started connecting to everything... Every single being within my surroundings. During that time, I also learned that colon cancer "ran in my family..." I set out on a quest to understand the physical, emotional, and mental ailments within my maternal bloodline and vowed to dedicate my life to ending these systemic cycles. For myself and my children, I have greatly succeeded. Years after the diagnosis, I did find by the power of The Holy Spirit that I was actually "rooted." By the time I had my third annual colonoscopy, my doctors were so impressed at my remission, my colonoscopies had been reduced to 3 years each. I am now at a colonoscopy every five-years which will not be decreased in time span because of the potentiality of recurrence.*

*For the Muladhara kundalini, I had just finished a round of reiki on myself after spending some time in nature because I was having a tough emotional day of holding space for myself all day (my first reiki sensei who I attained one of my mastery levels with and mentor here to this day is the great Patricia Iyer of Boston, MA). I then was driving to pick my kids up from school when all of a sudden, I began to have my first full kundalini. Kundalini experiences can occur in smaller forms, but this was my first full energetic release and was a full-fledged orgasmic explosion... While I was driving. Ha!*

*The sensation was so intense that I had to pull over to a parking lot, get out of my car and kneeled sobbing with huge tears; the experience was so beautiful. I have had other experiences with kundalini but without a doubt I knew I had just experienced my first full blown kundalini awakening. I rejoiced with amazement and honor. Most of us as human beings do not have even one kundalini experience with the exception of sexual and sensual induced orgasms because of the way we have been programmed to live our lives, especially within Western cultures. Little did I know, they get bigger and better with healing and completion of karmic cycles and tests, but we will discuss more about that later.*

## TRAUMA TREATMENT OPTIONS:

- Breath work with Yoga root level postures. **Yoga is the link and the release to the emotional body. It is a lost art and is the only physical activity that directly correlates to release stored energy.**
- Sound healing
- Placing Hands over chakra center. (Learning the Reiki technique will help maximize and fully emphasize the effects of hands on healing)
- Conduct Intake and treatment in nature to help guide and process should energetic root or generational curse be present.
- Light/Color Healing
- Ask for assistance from God, The Universe, and spirit guides.

Re-awakening is the deep knowledge that truly lies within each of us to allow everyone space to win. All over the world leaders, teachers, guides, and catalysts of the awakening process are awakening and springing into purpose. As a species we've learned the lessons needed to ascend our human species back to Unified Consciousness.

*"We may not always remember what a person said or did, but we will always remember how a person made us feel" -Ascended Master, Maya Angelou.*

Angels are referenced in all historical of spiritual belief and they are critical when it comes to a spiritual awakening. There are hundreds of angels, but these angels or the tangible aspects of the emotional impacts they help to govern within our lives, calling on them, will help us heal in deeper capacities. In every single story of the beginning of time, even the Bible which as a parable only depicts one species start as the human species. Angels were depicted in so many ways in so many cultures globally that it is impossible to cover their existence up. In western cultures, the knowledge, wisdom, and guidance these celestial bodies provide has been suppressed in an effort to keep humanity functioning from a third dimensional root level energy which is how we are continued to be enslaved.

Angels are referenced in many cultures as angels, Dakini, great winged beings, guardians of light, guides and more. Arch Angels are the highest in rank in analogous relationship to the "god" status energies. Their functions are assigned by the creator as the emissaries (ambassadors) of light. The topics of angels, guides, ancestors, ascended masters, etc. is a course within itself, but for the purpose of trauma recovery, we will be introduced to a few angels by name and function and hopefully create stable lasting relationships with them as they help us facilitate healing for our clients.

Why angels and guides? The work we conduct can be hard and heavy. For many supporting reasons we have the option to have direct contact with our team of guidance to help us better understand, interpret, and communicate not just for our clients' needs but also our own needs which helps us to be of better service to humanity. The timeline we are in now calls for us as lightworkers to bring human consciousness to new and higher levels of understanding as we work in conjunction with these celestial beings to bring human consciousness back to where we are intended to be. Again, we are ascending the planet and everything on it from a $3^{rd}$ dimensional understanding, which correlates to our soul star chakra, to a $5^{th}$ dimensional level of consciousness which correlates to the heart chakra. Fun fact, most of our human consciousness has the ability to function up to a $9^{th}$ dimensional level of consciousness without having to transcend. Unfortunately, while living, most humans do not exceed the $3^{rd}$ dimension. With the guidance of our soul teams, celestial beings, and our ancestors, we are here today to help turn the tide for us and future generations to come.

Arch angel Sandolphon (and his team of holy spirits) is the angel that guards over the earth subsequently our Muladhara, presents prayers to God, and directs the music in heaven. It is believed that Sandolphon had the rare appointment to incarnate on earth as the Prophet Elijah. This statement made in connection to Sandolphon sums up not only Sandolphon but the exact reason why it is beneficial to tie guidance back to healing emotional traumas.

*"Sandolphon brings grounding to your spiritual practice and Sandolphon's spiritual help is valuable for unifying the whole self by releasing the energy of alienation and fragmentation"*
*– Hazel Raven.*

CHAPTER THREE

# INTRODUCTION TO THE TREE OF LIFE

*"We cannot selectively numb emotions. When we numb the painful emotions, we also numb the positive emotions."*
*– Unknown.*

Our lives as fully functioning beings are inherently meant to be lives of balance and fulfillment. Our emotional balance begins within our exposure and experiences. **When we get beyond the suffering of our traumas, our lives come into pure balance and suffering subsides.** This is why this work matters… To us all. There are a lot of people who are looking for knowledge of self, which is amazing to know your culture and understand where you came from. But not many are given the resources as to why and this is what this works aims to do.

The Svadhisthana, sacral chakra, is our 2nd chakra and is located in our lower abdomen and navel area. Many say this energy point is located about 2 inches below the navel, however in my own practice, I find that this energy body can vary from person to person. Using the navel as a center is a good option because of this. The Svadhisthana is the central energetic channel that connects everything about you! It is the yin and yang of each of us containing our masculine and feminine potentials when in proper function is the dynamic that brings balance to our lives. It is the sole source of sensuality (a feminine pleasure equal to masculine sexuality), is the sole resource for our ability to feel and relate to joy and is the primary source for our creativity.

The Svadhisthana is the home of the emotional body connecting to each of our energetic ports and connects the body's meridian energy channels succinctly. We will discuss the body's meridian channels in the next chapters. Remember don't jump ahead. Let's have the full experience. You will either be enlightened or enhanced no matter what. While the functions of this chakra help to bring and maintain balance to our lives releasing the degrees of polarity, it is also the primary energy source for our utero and testicle regions within male and female genders. Much of the world today has been vastly oppressed within the vast capabilities of full range and scope of this chakra.

As a part of the repair of the unified consciousness grid to help close out the 13,000 year cycle, during the great time of our genre's shift in evolution from male dominance to the feminine alliance and persuasion, the work to prepare the female aspect of the grid began with the same group of Aboriginal descendants in and around 1987. The female aspect of the grid is the aspect that has been the most manipulated keeping the male species the dominant gender. The primary physical locations of this energy are located on the island of Moorea and Egypt, and there are about forty other locations on earth holding the points of energy included as a part of the grid's reparation connected to the feminine consciousness.

## CREATION/CREATIVITY. THE PERSONALITY

Remember the saying, "As above, so below"? That is true in all aspects of life. Within our planet, there are energetic portals throughout the world that hold the power and domain to each of these energy portals much like we will later discuss within our internal meridian system. We will also discuss more about energy portals and energy domains when we discuss the solar plexus and the crown chakra functions.

In relation to the Svadhisthana, we will discuss the tree of life. Why on earth would we do that here? With a blocked or low functioning Svadhisthana, we are more likely to experience the following as part of the breakdown of our personality.

- Seductive Patterns
- Illness Seducing Entities/Imbalanced Bacteria
- Addiction Seducing Entities
- Grudges/Jealousy
- Promiscuity
- Depression
- Personality Disorders
    - Narcissism, Border-Personality Disorder, Sociopath, Paranoia, Antisocial, Etc.

**We have an anointing over our lives and if we conduct ourselves according to our purpose, not in comparison to others, we will find the most joy in life possible.** The tree of life is the trinity that gives our emotional body the premise of our personality. It is our very own written emotional purpose.

It is responsible for our kundalini energy which is what really allows us to function in full alignment. Kundalini is not bad as so many of us were taught to believe. That is another piece of the program. As we move through each sephira in our level of consciousness, our energy moves with it, and we are able to expand our consciousness and do even more! I suspect that one day modern science will be able to read a DNA strand and provide detailed information that directly correlates to the same information we find in astrology and can appropriately read the purpose/life plan of our species. I can say that I 'know' this does not yet exist. But, I'm sure it will.

The paths are the link to our soul's evolution. The sephira represents the aspects of our personality we are learning from to attain the highest level of consciousness possible. It is replicated throughout time and space applying to every living thing. The tree of life is depicted as two solid pillar energetic channels with one single opaque energy channel through the middle. The paths are the steppingstones to our soul's achievements and triumphs for our life journey and are, "The Creators" plan hardcoded into our emotional bodies for our soul's maximum growth along our journey. You can consider them to be a checkpoint or like a map that will guide us to our soul's highest level of evolution. In many cases in trauma, many individuals get stuck on one path and don't exceed to the next journey or soul lesson because they are left wounded and are stuck in flight or fight mode emotionally. This is why this is important. Understanding what you are meant to accomplish and when, will help enlighten your soul and create clear energy flows within your emotional bodies. Essentially, understanding this subject in itself, is exactly what yoga does for our emotional body.

Within these three columns, are ten primary spheres called sephiroth. Sephiroth is further connected with about thirty-two various interconnected lines called paths. I believe that as we are evolving as a species, these paths are increasing. Just as we as the human species are being found to currently be growing new DNA strands. (Currently doctors and researchers have reported finding DNA strands that now consist of 4-5 strands within a single DNA pod which is an increase of the former teachings of the 2-strand model.) The paths we know of currently, represent the twenty letters in the Hebrew alphabet, representing our subjective conscious and our conscious personalities. The Kabbalah describes the tree of life as the second in all creation after the, "Infinite Light."

They are further broken down based on the day we are born, down to the hour, minute, and location of birth. They are the, "Ten Holy Emanations" and have been later translated to the original Ten Commandants to provide further interpretation of each sephiroth's true and deeper meaning. Because so much of humanity operates from the root chakra, many people believe they have the right to the will of choice in this dimension. It is my belief that this acceptance and push for self-will is what keeps our souls as a species tied to the death and rebirth cycle here in this dimension. The truth is, because we helped create this plan, the will of our Divine Creator Elohim, is in fact the will that aligns with each and every one of us. The tree of life is representative in its full operating capacity of personality traits of Christ Consciousness and in physical action as the balanced swing of the pendulum.

## THE TREE IS COMPRISED OF:
1. Left pillar
   b. Judgment
   c. Femininity
   d. Passivity
   e. Understanding (The third sphere of the Tree- 3)
   f. Judgement or Severity (The fifth sphere- 5)
   g. Glory (The eighth sphere- 8)

2. Middle Pillar
   a. Equilibrium
   b. Mildness
   c. Crown (The first sphere- 1)
   d. Beauty (The sixth sphere- 6)
   e. Foundation (The ninth sphere- 9)
   f. Kingdom (The tenth sphere- 10)

3. Right Pillar
   a. Mercy
   b. Masculinity
   c. Wisdom (The second sphere- 2)
   d. Mercy or Love (The fourth sphere- 4)
   e. Victory (The seventh sphere- 7)

As individuals we each pass through these spheres in series to our soul's highest and best path of evolution again and can be further calculated based on the date, time, and location of our birth. The similarities in the DNA strand and the tree of life are uncanny and cannot possibly be a mistake.

# TREE OF LIFE PILLARS AND SPHERES

The pillar of mercy ascribes to the masculine/positive qualities, the left pillar to judgement or severity/negative or "kethode" qualities (referencing Hermetic principles), and the middle are the central transmitters to each sphere and holds an androgynous denote. The principles of yoga have been built off of these three pillar's representations and resulted in the yoga arts of Ida, Shusumna, and Pingala. Within each chapter we will discuss the relative sphere for chakra purposes as they relate to our emotional bodies. The Muladhara/Root chakra is correlated to the sphere of # 10- Kingdom which translates to the formal name Malkuth.

## MALKUTH/KINGDOM/ SEPHIROTH #10

Malkuth is the emanation of the material world. The root chakra, the earthly third dimension. It is the kingdom and the foundation. It is known as, "The Queen, the Inferior Mother, the Bride of the Macroprosopos and the Shekinah." More associations to Malkuth are, "Gate of Death, Gate of the Garden of Eden, and the virgin." The God name associated to this sphere is Adonai Ha Aretz and the Arch Angel is Arch Angel Sandolphon. Malkuth is the sphere of the physical body and its matter is solid, gas, and liquid. The angelic realm of its association is the Ashim realm, which is created by the souls of fire.

*Adonai* is a plural word which correlates further to master, ruler, and has concepts of dominion, rulership, and ownership. In understanding the interpretation of God as *Adonai*, we are representing God as Malkuth, our provider, protector, guard, lord of lords, leader, and all things pertaining to the physical functions and emotional aspects of the Muladhara/root chakra/

the 10th sephira on the tree of life. *Adonai* is the aspect of surrender sephira Malkuth through the Muladhara, which is the process of the 'unveiling.' The first step in the process to attaining human evolution.

# YESOD

This sephira is the 9$^{th}$. Its location is also the middle pillar, the pillar of Equilibrium and is the connection to the union of the sephira Hod/Glory the 8$^{th}$ and Netzach/Victory the 7$^{th}$. We will discuss the specific functions of these two sephiras in the solar plexus chapters. Yesod's God name is Shaddai El Chai which translates to the Almighty Living God. It is important to note that we are not referencing different God archetypes within these titles, merely different aspects of the Divine creator of all things, Elohim. The Arch Angel presiding over this sephira and the Svadhisthana, sacral chakra is Arch Angel Gabriel. The angelic order, angelic guides and realm are the ceribum. Yesod associates to the moon, the negative, kethoed, and feminine properties of the human species but in this representation is depicted more as a unifying sephira. Its primary function is the action of purification and can be associated to the planet Mercury.

The lunar tides, and flow of water are all maintained within the function of this sephira/realm. Replicating functions from the God source of energy flow, to the rhythm and law of the universe to the flow and law of the human species. Water, the tides, and our bodily fluids, menstrual cycles, and the ejaculation of the epididymis (sperm storage) are all controlled by the magnetic force produced within the sephira of Yesod. *El Shaddai* in this representation is the aspect of covenant. No matter what our spiritual preference is, it is this union of this sephira's meaning of purification that provides this level of connection to *El Shaddai*. For further reference, *El Shaddai* is the aspect of God that is depicted within the Biblical story of Abram. The aspect of *El Shaddai* as it relates to Yesod through the Svadhisthana is the constant supply of nourishment.

## PATHWAYS OF MALKUTH AND YESOD.

Pathways of the tree of life that connect Malkuth and Yesod in relation to function to one another are 28, 29, 30, 31, and 32:

- Path 32- recognized as 'Administrative Intelligence' this path directs all operations of the seven planets within our solar system, (Pluto is no longer considered a planet), our 7 sephira of the tree of life, and our seven emotional body chakras.
- Path 31- recognized as 'Perpetual Intelligence' This path regulates the 'motions' of both the sun and moon, masculine and feminine, positive and negative charges, sustaining balance between and appropriate orbit of the energies.
- Path 30- connects Hod and Malkuth. Known as 'Collecting Intelligence' associates the aspect of judgement and reason. Traditionally ancient astrologers recognized this path as the aspect of perfection.
- Path 29- 'Corporeal Intelligence' Takes the physical aspect of the body and applies it to creation. This path, "Forms everybody beneath the whole set of worlds and the increments of them."

- Path 28- The path of Netzach and Yesod. This path has no aforementioned definition, based on my studies of the tree of life in relation to chakra and emotional body functions, I'd say this path is related to balance, unity of masculine and feminine qualities, and the yin yang aspects to development. Its formal description is probably missing for obvious reasons, but this part of our evolution is encouraging us to each embrace and heal the masculine and feminine qualities within each of us.

## HERMETIC LAW

The Hermetic law that applies to the Svadhisthana, sacral chakra is the law of Repetition: The Microcosm and Macrocosm. This law recognizes that each system within existence, form, time, and motion to man, planet, and solar system hold the same functioning within each of the body, plant, and constellation. The law of repetition recognizes that there is in fact an "order" to the structure of life to each and every being. Meaning... our experiences are in fact divinely orchestrated. The earth itself depicts this law perfectly as our Mother Earth has two poles of energetic access ports running through it as the North pole, the masculine positive charge and the South pole the feminine magnetic charge. The properties and flow of these two energies exists in replica and continues on to infinity.

We will listen to the properties of the law of Polarity in the Hermetic principles of the Kybalion together as it relates to the function of the Svadhisthana.

With this knowledge, at this point of emotional enlightenment, each individual has the choice to impose their own earthly will for self-indulgence and sexual influence, or to participate in the flow and the law of creation as we assisted in design in a state of surrender. The Svadhisthana connects to our Mental Body within our auric field and reflects the color/ray orange. The Mental Body that surrounds it is that in which corresponds to our emotional body and also sends signals and communicates our emotions to our mind. The Etheric Body is where the telepathic thought is communicated and translated.

In relation to functioning for the Muladhara root chakra, the Physical Body is what allows us to recognize physical objects that vibrate at similar frequencies and gives us the functioning reality of our third dimensional existence.

CHAPTER FOUR

# THE BODY'S 7 MAJOR SYSTEMS

**IN RESPECT TO** what we've already covered, we will discuss the additional systems as they correlate to the emotional body and each point of energy throughout the chakra system. I'm sure a scientific review will support the finding if adequately researched. This information may in fact be the link to the scientific pursuit of understanding the hypothesis 'why.' The emotional body is the missing link.

In my opinion, by next understanding the emotional body by connecting the dots to the varying resources available and fully unlocking and understanding the human energetic emotional body, is a great link to the pathway of human evolution. Science accounts for six major body systems. There are nine, but for now we will add one making the course of this understanding a total of seven. I am going to attach each of the major systems to the appropriate chakra based on relative functionality beginning at the root. How do I know? I've done it over and over again first, beginning with myself and then my children and then I moved on to my clients and close friends. However, there are some individuals that do not ascend the Muladhara stage of human consciousness (no judgement on my part). Although some have disconnected, there are many who stay on the same vibrational wavelength and we continue our evolution together as soul family.

# THIS IS A LISTING OF THE MAJOR BODY SYSTEMS AND THE CHAKRA CONNECTION EACH CORRELATE TO:

1. Skeletal System- Muladhara/Root Chakra
2. Emotional/Chakra System- Svadhisthana/Sacral Chakra (This is the body system I am adding for context).
3. Nervous System- Manipura/Solar Plexus
4. Muscular System- Anahata/ Heart Chakra
5. Digestive System- Vishuddha/Throat Chakra
6. Circulatory System- Ajna/ Third Eye Chakra
7. Respiratory System- Sarhasrara/Crown Chakra

The skeletal system gives us our structure. Its density creates the third dimensional reality we live in and all that we perceive in this level of consciousness can be correlated to the physical realm. The Muladhara/Root Chakra is responsive to this layer of existence.

## THE EMOTIONAL BODY

This system is the balance of the physical and energetic realms and consists of auric fields, our chakras, and our meridians. It is the perception of vibration and the frequencies matching those of the human eye's perception of a rainbow. All that we are learning about within this context.

## NUMBERS AND THE EMOTIONAL BODY

Have you ever asked yourself what is a number? Seriously, let's consider that... Is it actually a glandular system that provides value from varying degrees of less and more? Or are they in fact the varying degrees of frequency within a pendulum's swing? Numbers hold a vibrational frequency in themselves that allow us in every way shape and form to place a value to an object's positioning. How is it possible that numbers also equate to alphabetical values and to the sephiras on the tree of life, DNA, soul path, and fully map out the values of greater or less? Numbers are actually every single thing ever! Numbers and math are often referred to in philosophers' circles as the science of God/the creator. Understanding numbers is a whole new topic in itself. For this topic, trauma recovery and for further understanding I'll discuss the most popular references to numerology. The connection to the higher self. Because of the electric universe we are a part of, the magnetic force brings the universe into balance.

"As above. So below" Right? It is believed in the woo woo world of which I humbly subscribe, that we are one version of ourselves here on earth. It is believed that there are aspects of ourselves in other dimensions of time space reality. Like the movie Avatar. Some say we are dormant beings in other dimensional reality (which I can see) or some say that we are fully conscious beings waiting to be fully caught up and that life as we know it has already existed because time does not really exist. Whatever you choose to believe, is your right. But from my experience, we receive messages via varying different resources within this experience as a human soul.

For this context we will discuss two. The first, our higher selves and secondly our spirit guides/angelic team. These numbers let us know where we are with respect to our path and our destiny, further unlock our personal sephira's meaning to subconscious souls on a personal level and provide general guidance to the path we are taking by providing us with confirmation from Holy Spirits. For this context the following is a brief demonstration of number interpretation:

## HIGHER SELF:

According to teachings of the Nakaal School of Mastery (Drunvalo Melchizedek)

111- Energy Flow- Any flow of energy electricity, money, emotions, water, sexual energy, etc.

222- New Cycle- The beginning of a new cycle. (Associates to any other triple number.)

333- Decision- You have a decision to make. If your decision leads you to the number 666, you will have to repeat the cycle over. (Karma)

444- Learning about how to relate your spiritual experiences to reality. Learning.

555- Unified Consciousness. Mastery of one subject. Five is the number of Christ.

666- Earth Consciousness. This is the number of the mark of the beast and karmic cycles.

777- Learning and practicing life. The number of 'God'

888- Completion of a soul lesson.

999- Completion of a life cycle.

## ANGEL NUMBERS:

111- Represents spiritual awakening. Your angels and guides want you to pay close attention.

1111- Symbolizes that there is an energetic connection and flow between you and divine love of varying sources.

222- Encouragement to continue with your faith. Angels are working on your behalf.

333- Your prayers are being answered and what you are praying for is being delivered.

444- You are were you need to be, and your angels and guides are ready to assist.

555- Positive change is among you.

777- Increase in spiritual growth. God number and means you are on the right path

888- Accomplishments and abundance are among you.

999- Completion- graduation, something in your life is completing.

711- Combines the vibration of 7 and 1 and encourages one to start over, move forward, and chase individual goals.

911- Call to follow your destiny and divine calling.

311- Happiness and peace of mind. Encourages to follow the heart.

144- An important message of passion, energy, commitment, and recognition.

# SVADHISTHANA/SACRAL CHAKRA

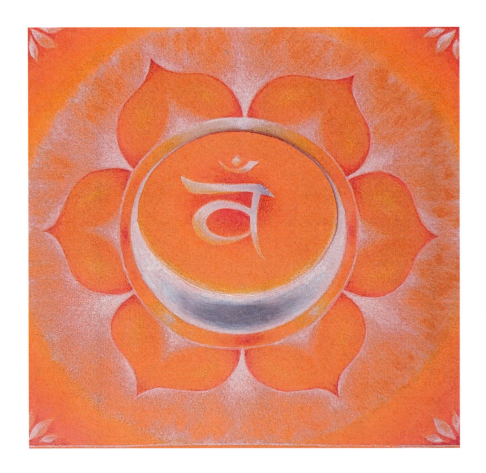

## SVADHISTHANA

This chakra is located at the start of the navel area and could reside anywhere within 2-3 inches below. The following statement sums up the fully awakened sacral chakra in all of its full capacity.

*"The first essential to health, therefore, is to believe—to believe in ourselves, our power over ourselves and our destinies. The second is to recognize that we are meant to be happy."*
– Vera Staley Adler 'The finding of the third eye.'

This book was the very first I read when I had my full spiritual awakening. I had gone through a massive dark night of the soul that was around relationships, medical concerns, and constant transition. Within reading the first three pages of this book I was reciting to myself, "How did I know that?" over and over again. I strongly recommend it. For context, my business partner in Day Seven Wellness Center, Vare Raymond, has been witness to my entire healing journey. We have always remained close. Always. Emotionally, he is the most mature person I know. He has been my personal psychologist and I have been his philosopher. I shared this information with him and from the jump he was all ears. Spiritually and pertaining to my gifts and abilities, he knows most things about me. There are some things about my gifts and spiritual nature that I have not shared yet. Patiently awaiting approval. I reread 'The Finding of the Third Eye' once in a while and it's always a treasure.

Our Svadhisthana is everything about who we are. It holds and processes the various codes and all that is written within our destiny. Everything about the sacral chakra is about you. How we treat it determines how our personalities shape. The sacral chakra sends energy and provides strength to every chakra above it all the way up to the crown. This is the center that holds the yin yang to our lives and all that we are. I know I've been repetitive, but I think the functions of the sacral chakra are not often spoken about within this level of depth. The sacral chakra's primary role is:

- Uterus
- Testicles
- Kidneys
- Bladder
- Circulatory System
- Nervous System
- Sciatic Nerve
- Proactively drives and influences all other chakras

This is quite the task. A healthy functioning Svadhisthana, sacral chakra, is going to give us strong self-worth, healthy relationships, healthy boundaries, joy, laughter, creativity, and spontaneity. Traumas include:

1. Sexual Abuse
2. Emotional Abuse
3. Violence
4. Neglect
5. Codependency
6. Overbearing
7. Love based on control or domination
8. Etc.

This is a LOT to learn about how to treat a blocked sacral. The most influential impact to the Svadhisthana is water. In all forms and in every single way we use water. The amount of water we drink, bathing and swimming. ponds, rivers, lakes, and oceans. Bodily Fluids. The rain. And each one of them can have the combination to help aid additional chakras. Yes, water does in fact represent birth, replenishment, and rebirth. It is a baptismal force. The sound frequency that correlates to the sacral is around 303HZ-606HZ. This frequency protects the auric field, the emotional body as well as the energetic ties we are meant to securely hold. The color that correlates to the Svadhisthana is orange.

## MICROBIOMES

Microbiomes are bacteria that each of us have. Among the many kinds of bacteria, we hold as a species alone, microbiomes play a very big role. The primary shelter within our bodies housing these bacteria are within our intestines, however, there have been reports that show that they also live in our mouths, skin, vagina, and placenta. Their sole function is to balance the hormonal exchange in the related microbiome. Microbiome is affected in many ways throughout our lives and can impact our immune systems and for the subject matter of this material, the signals our Svadhisthana sends to our brain. Our emotional body is predominantly controlled by the sacral, and further connects our internal energy flows. The microbiome is a replica of our personalities. It holds the same energy we omit. Character traits such as introversion or extroversion apply in accordance to how we feel about anything.

Studies have shown that microbiomes that are exchanged between similar living species take on the character trait once the exchange of microbiomes is completed and either subject do in fact assume the alternative personality. Interestingly enough, I'd push this to further hypothesize that they are also contagious and can be exchanged within subject to subject as well like a virus. Microbiomes can be produced within our choices for nourishment as well. As we can all imagine, those impacts can be extraordinarily impactful working with us to our highest and best or they can tear us down.

We are what we eat. Each substance we consume has a vibrational frequency and application of sacred geometry of its own. We even assume the dormant energy and emotions of the environment of the food we consume through our Svadhisthana. These energies are being processed at an unconscious level. Imagine how much energy we as beings are actually taking in. Shortly, we are going to conduct a meditation to bring our unconscious thought forms to realization, but before we do, let us discuss the social psychology theories that impact the Svadhisthana.

CHAPTER FIVE

# Social Psychology

1. Schemata Theory: Schemas or bias that lead to a bias in memory and how they perceive a situation. Experiences that are stored within our brains, then become the guidelines for future experiences with similar circumstances. Essentially, this is the theory that we see most when our clients are stuck in cyclical occurrences.
2. Drive Theory: Is the motivation that dictates specific behaviors and creates a cycle within individuals that makes a first experience bias. This theory dictates how future experiences occur from the vantage point of the client.
3. Attribution Theory: This is the rationalization of the behaviors of others which is an internal to external process. From the internal perspective it references personality, ability, and exertions. Externally we will see this theory play out in triggers, weather, associates, social standing, money, or pressure.

**TAKE A MOMENT** to identify if you or anyone you know subscribes to these theories. Chances are if these qualities are identifiable, then clearings can be done to help release stored energy and bring balance to an overarching thought process.

Take a moment to document any key phrases, catch statements or actions we may identify when consulting our clients that would directly correlate to root chakra blockages.

| Key Phrases | Catch Statements | Actions |
|---|---|---|
|  |  |  |
|  |  |  |
|  |  |  |
|  |  |  |
|  |  |  |

An imbalanced Svadhisthana will cause an individual to suffer from depression primarily, but will demonstrate itself through anger, violence, jealousy, emotional paralysis, infertility, and a lack of creativity where there once was. Let's conduct our unconscious mind meditation to see what our unconscious mind communicates to bring to the surface for a focal point.

Here's the promised meditation: http://bit.ly/soiwokeup-eradicateguiltnfear

## CORDING

In my early pursuit to understand what cording is and how its impacts, I came across an interesting subject in relation to it by Mary Shutan. Mary introduced the concept of energetic hygiene as her explanation of Cording. Within the systemic relationship energy fields of which there are many, we each have an energetic cord to the people we associate with or come in acquaintance to. Ideally these cords are healthy links to energetic vibrations creating healthy and self-sustaining relationships. **Energy Hygiene as described by Mary Shutan is an implementation of practices and tools to help maintain our physical body and energy as our own.**

Most of us go through life without the realization that this actually exists and some who are well aware of it, even if they don't know the formal terms for the functions involved, while others will use this process to their own advantage. Sexual intercourse is actually also an act of Cording. You will cord energetically to every sexual partner you encounter, and this is where promiscuity becomes tricky. Some people cord energetically without sex to another person and do not even know they are doing it. This is done through jealousy, idolization, worship, codependency, obsession, etc. It is important for us as lightworkers that we understand this concept so that we know where our client's energy is coming from. Cording can be interrelated to soul ties.

Cording is the link to genetic disease and emotional dysfunction. Magically, this method is conducted through the use of string and ribbon. Although, I am not formally versed in the actual process, I am aware of how to break the energy. Again, I personally do not practice magic or anything that forces another soul to operate outside of their own will or destiny. Please bear with me, you will see that I reference this stance often as to not have my guidance misconstrued.

Because the topic of cording is vast in subject matter, we will keep the topic to as minimal coverage as possible so we can get to the overarching goal of producing healthy energetic flows through the Svadhisthana. Cords exist in an essentially psychic manner and those of us who are not fully functioning in our sacral oftentimes cord to another individual creating a pattern of codependency. We also see this on the latter, which is the form I had personally suffered from, and do not allow anyone to cord to me as a result of unpleasant experiences within past relationships. I'll share my experience later in my testimony. The only people who should be corded to us in our adult lives are our children and balanced committed exchanges. And, in my opinion, not beyond the point where those energetic links are not sustainable. Cords create a gain, loss, or balance of energy. The goal here is balance. Malicious use of cording will attempt to drain or control the energy port through which the exertion, knowingly or unknowingly, is being created.

Cording ultimately creates a loss of balance within our energetic productivity and can create the following reactions:

- Substance Abuse
- Lack of desire
- Loss in interest of sexual interaction
- Fatigue
- Loss of Focus and creativity

This is where our choice in relationships matters the most. Cording is an uninvited act to another. This is a tie that binds us even without our consent. Meditation is the biggest resource we have against cording because proper meditation keeps us in a state of balance and keeps us alert to the varying energies that are attempting to attach to our auric fields. I will say, there are some cords that exist that are bonded to through a divine resource and are not meant to be broken. Trust me... I've tried to release a few that will not break. Cords exist in all time and space and can be altered in any form of existence.

I say to all clients I work with, especially the fellow clairsentients (one who has the ability to emotionally and physically *feel* other's emotions and feelings), that I meet that **being in your own energy is VERY important**. Cording can be done through any of our emotional body's energetic ports, but I find it most impacts the sacral area then secondly the Ajna/heart chakra and I think if we consider the functions of the Svadhisthana properly, we can clearly identify why and how.

Because the sacral chakra largely connects to our brain functions, cording uses the emotional body's auric field to alter the state of our emotional responses by manipulating the triggered response desired through telepathic interference. Cording being done through malice uses the feelings and emotions of another to achieve the 'corder's' desired outcomes. Through a process of meditation if you can identify a feeling/emotion of which you have no connection to or an origination to, chances are there is an energetic cord that can be released. I conduct a mediation that you can also be used with your clients should you feel an energetic cording is taking place to identify any cords that need to be released. Feel free to visit my website to learn more here: https://www.daysevenwellnesscenter.com/

## SPIRITUAL GIFTS

The gifts that connect with our fully functioning Svadhisthana is telepathy. **Telepathy is the communication of thoughts or ideas by the senses in our emotional bodies**. Many philosophers and scientists or practitioners will correlate this ability to the crown chakra area, which is in fact true, but I've hypothesized and proven through my own experiences and knowledge that telepathy actually in fact starts at the sacral chakra. Telepathy is one of my strongest gifts. Please know that I do not walk around intentionally reading minds or imposing any of my spiritual gifts (I have unlocked dozens of them) on anyone. I am more focused on living my own life and learning what I am meant to learn in my life and help to teach anyone who is willing to learn.

**But, my ability to communicate telepathically has taught me a gift about understanding the human process and totally understand that others are where they are and it is not our job to correct, dictate, or subsequently feel any type of way about where another person is on their journey.** To use this gift without detriment to our own internal process of growth or to help aid in another's, we will best function from a stance of non-judgement. If you are still in a state of judgement no matter what the reason, telepathy could do more harm than good if it comes from an unhealed space, and I just want everyone to win.

You may feel that you are imagining things, but telepathy is our ability to inwardly hear and/or feel the thoughts, feelings, and emotions of others. Telepathy is one of the most prominent extensions of clairsentience. Telepathy is connected to Clairsentience which gives a physical feeling 'gut feeling', 'something doesn't feel right.' It gives you the same sensation of that which is transmitting the energy. Clairsentience applies to all living matter and a very well-developed clairsentient (empath) can and will connect to physical and emotional reactions to animals, trees and plants, other human beings, etc. I myself often times feel the emotional responses of others and it was a task to keep that under wraps. I 'feel' when others are having feelings of indifference with me or with themselves and projecting their feelings on to me and I've taught many others who have this innate developed gift to do the same, however with an individual who is still determined to operate through the self-will as opposed to the will of unified consciousness, they have the potential to continue to impose negative self-projections on others and just begin do it in an educated way although the energy still does not evade.

You can also block telepathy. Some knowingly or unknowingly persist a block, but again, some are unaware of how this process works. Please don't rush to assume that you are under a psychic or energetic attack or cording because that is not always the case. Some people are merely getting adjusted to the ability. To block telepathy, you can do so through a visual meditation and give yourself a symbol of sorts that associates to your ideal energetic ports. My personal symbol is a heavy ornate door or my connection to my astral body/higher self. When I feel someone entering my space energetically that I do not agree with, for any reason, I close the door or turn my astral back as if to suggest, 'not now.' And for the same reason, I request permission to communicate telepathically with another if I need to with someone else. Some who are also telepathically gifted see and feel this interaction. The feedback I've received is remarkable and undeniable. It is rare that someone persists beyond that, but if they do, become firmer.

## TRAUMA TREATMENT OPTIONS:

- Breath work with yoga combined through root and sacral chakra level postures. Yoga is the link and the release to the emotional body. It is a lost art and is the only physical activity that directly correlates to release stored energy.
- Cord Cutting
- Sound healing
- Placing Hands over chakra center. (Learning Reiki, Tapping, or Kinesiology techniques will help maximize and fully emphasize the effects of hands on healing especially for sacral work)

- Conduct Intake and treatment in nature to help guide and process should an energetic root or generational curse be present.
- Light/Color Healing
- Ask for assistance from God, The Universe, and spirit guides.
- Muscle Testing
    - Because muscle testing is a kinesiology tool and works with the polarity forces of yes and no, I will discuss the practice here. There are several types of muscle testing that we can conduct. Doctors utilize this practice with varying techniques and tools, and I suspect that some utilize the self-muscle testing for their patients as well. For trauma response, we are going to discuss two specific types of muscle testing that I'd recommend and one additional one for fun. Using your own frequency and polarity your body can help aid in simple yes or no answers. Why would this work well with a client? Let's use Mrs. V. as another example. A client like Mrs. V., who isn't very expressive, may need a little more support about the types of trauma recovery techniques we can use to help her. Pendulums also work by applying the same laws of polarity. We can apply this tool to anything we do, but like with anything else, we want to make sure we do not abuse the tool to manipulate our will over anything.

1. Latch your fingers together to form an infinity symbol with your thumb and your index fingers together like an interlocking pinch that creates the infinity symbol. Keep your left fingers pointed up and your right fingers pointed down. Ask your body to show you 'yes' and give your fingers as they are interlocked a gentle tug. For most people, your fingers will slip right through. For your no you will be the opposite of the initial response. I am one of the rare responses. My fingers slide through on yes and stop on no. Give it try. I hope that worked for you. If it didn't keep trying and stay relaxed. It will.
2. The next technique is more discrete but isn't as clear unless you have a habit of conducting it. Place your fingers on your dominant writing hand together as if you were to snap. I recommend using your index finger and your thumb only, but you can incorporate your middle finger as well. Ask your body again to show you 'yes' and 'no.' Take your time with it so that you can notice the obvious change in the responses your body gives you.
3. * For fun. This method is effective however, you will look silly doing it. Standing with your feet shoulder width apart and your arms by your side with your palms facing forward again, ask your body to show you 'yes' and 'no.' The response will be that your body will lean slightly forward either forward or back for yes and in the opposite direction for no.

This isn't a requirement but is an extra tool to help you troubleshoot trauma relief strategies for your clients. This works especially well with the Svadhisthana as the law of polarity largely applies. Again, our chakras can identify trauma through blockage just as well as over activity or an overstimulated chakra. The more tools we have to help our clients the better, right?

## PERSONAL TESTIMONY

*My sacral chakra has always been pretty active. But like most of us I have had my challenges with it. My sacral at varying times has been blocked and at most other times, it has been overactive. Let me first talk about the blockage. When I was a small child all of my senses and my spiritual gifts were active and budding like many children, but I was a little more expressive with mine than most. The day before my 11th birthday (which was the year I experienced the most threshold trauma in my childhood), I went to Hampton Beach with a friend and her family. While visiting an arcade and playing a game, I was snatched, and a man attempted to abduct me. He snatched my arm and started to try to pull me with him. In that moment I froze and stood as stiff as I possible could with my eyes squeezed shut.*

*I could feel every single emotion that was happening around me including his. I felt a weird sensation throughout that I knew came from him that I could not and still cannot identify with today, but I knew it was him. I felt my childhood friend panic with fear. I had this experience several times before but for the most part it was associated to love or joy never trauma. I could actually feel exactly what they were feeling in my friend's chest and in the pit of the perpetrator's stomach but could not feel myself. This scared me.*

*The rest of the night, while at the police station participating in the lineup identification process and waiting for my family to arrive from the next state over time seemed to float by as if I were witnessing myself in a dream. I stayed quiet and reserved for weeks after that experience and I had a difficult time releasing the emotional memory of feeling that man's emotions although I did not know how to identify it at the time. I shut my clairsentience down after that, which in retrospect probably helped me get through that year. I was also molested during that year and I have no clue what I would've experienced if I had actually also felt the feelings and emotions of the perpetrator of that act.*

*I did not fully release the intentional block I placed on my sacral chakra until many years later when I became pregnant with my first child. Prior to my pregnancy, I never let another living soul get that emotionally close to me again for the mere fact that I would feel the emotions someone else was feeling while I was being violated. It feels good to be able to put words to it today. I overcompensated the blockage by swinging hard to the opposite spectrum of the chakra use and my creative abilities skyrocketed. Unfortunately for most women who have like experiences, they become promiscuous and lose their self-worth. On the latter, I buried myself in sports and my creative efforts and was reluctant to really connect to anyone although I fully expected to receive but could not fully give. To anyone who had this dysfunctional experience with me, I have since apologized for my shortcomings. I didn't know any better back then.*

*In all those years I held on to the emotion I felt and did not allow myself to acknowledge my own emotions after the shock of being able to feel others in that moment so immensely until I went through my inner child healing process with vigorous 1:1 therapy soon after I gave birth to my second son and to heal my issues with my colon and reproductive system. I had been tested a few times at that point for personality disorders and each came back clear with the exception to a diagnosis of PTSD. I went through a process called EMDR which allows you to acknowledge your feelings to fully feel them and then allows you to disassociate from the trauma through a process that recalibrates your neurological wiring to the trauma. It worked wonders.*

*A few years later, after meditation and a full day of outward worship and singing and chanting and prayer, I burst into fits of genuine laughter. I had the spirit laugh and I knew it was my kundalini awakening for my Svadhisthana. I was laughing so hard I was jumping up and down! About a week later, I was working with a client during a 1:1 session and my clairsentience kicked back in bigger and bolder than ever before. I could actually feel each of this client's emotional blockages and could describe and share the sensations my client was feeling. My client did not clearly identify the sensations until I brought them into awareness as they were emotions my client had deeply suppressed and learned to live with like so many of us do.*

*I went with the flow of the process of working with my client through a series of breathwork techniques to remove the blockages. My client was moved to an abundance of tears and joy (and a little bit of awkwardness) from the experience. In the years after this experience, I learned how to fully accept my gift* and the many arms of clairsentience and telepathy. I have also created various ways to eliminate the impact of the negative emotions from connecting to me... I can now stop the cording process before it occurs, for the most part anyway.

Today, I know if it does touch me or a client, there is a lesson in it for our growth. To block cording and like negative emotions, I use crystals (jets, black tourmaline, and black obsidian) and cord cutting meditations on a regular basis and not only does it help me not feel unwanted emotions that belong to others and are their emotions for them to explore in whatever way they see fit as long as they do not intend to inflict harm on me. I apply my clairsentient abilities to all that I do in a positive way. Channeling and Clairsentience is how I conduct and choreograph my yoga sessions allowing myself to fully connect with the feelings and emotions of others to help them clear blockages and heal.

The angel that presides over the Svadhisthana is Arch Angel Gabriel. Arch Angel Gabriel is one of two angels that is formally named within the Bible (there are hundreds and thousands of angels and holy spirits). Gabriel is famously known as the messenger that Mary would bare the seed of the Holy Spirit. Gabriel is the angel of communication and helps to encourage teachers, authors, and artists. Gabriel is the angel of purification. This angel helps in child conception, pregnancy and birth. Gabriel often provides messages through dreams. This Archangel has been depicted as both male and female and because of the androgynous ties to the sacral chakra, this makes sense.

Fun fact, the Aztec/Mayan Goddess Tlazolteotl, is believed to be the first female to physically give birth and also pro-

*vides influence on the Svadhisthana. Tlazolteotl, is the global symbol of Obstetrics and Gynecology. (Tlazolteotl is misinterpreted in modern times as abhorrent because she is translated as 'goddess of filth', but this is because she is known to purify souls, forgive sins, and cure epilepsy).*

# SECTION II

PERSONALITY DISORDERS
TREE OF LIFE
MERKABAH
STAR TETRAHEDRON
MERIDIANS
MANIPURA
SOLAR PLEXUS TRAUMA
HEXAGRAMS
WHAT IS YOGA?
BODY SYSTEMS
ANAHATA
SHAMBALA
HEART CHAKRA TRAUMA
SOCIAL PSYCHOLOGY
HEALING RESOURCES/ BREATHING TECHNIQUES

CHAPTER SIX

# PERSONALITY DISORDERS

**WAYNE DYER AND** many other energy healers and teachers have famously quoted, "We are not a body, but a body with a soul," but let's break this down, shall we? As a fall out of the Svadhisthana/sacral chakra and Muladhara root chakras, our conscious energy starts to unfold. The results of opening the unconscious mind, budding, or full blossoming energy flow of the root resolve varying impacts that could obstruct the functionality of the human soul, which is the subject matter of this module, the Manipura.

The Manipura is the chakra that starts our subconscious conscious state of being. The Manipura unlike our other chakras, relies heavily on its functionality of a flow of energy in a push pull fashion. Honest personality disorders (not misdiagnosed or generally categorized disorders) manifest themselves in our behaviors and the way that we respond to the world. They show themselves in our interests, in what we promote, in what we accept, etc. because they are what we have exposure to. It is the source of our personal power and the direct link to our soul. When we are shut down from a blocked or overactive Svadhisthana, our Manipura acts as a push and pushes the energy flow from the Svadhisthana outwardly. In our auric field this chakra correlates to our Mental Auric Body.

# MANIPURA/SOLAR PLEXUS CHAKRA

## PERSONALITY DISORDERS

Trauma is a major cause of personality disorders because of the breakdown trauma causes to the emotional body. Personality disorders are typically clinically broken down into three categories. **Personality disorders begin in the lower two chakra regions and manifest the emotional responses on the remaining chakras causing blockages which later lead to**

**medical complications in many cases or cause an overactive chakra that processes emotions in a projectile inward fashion.** As we know and I say all the time, we are all here suffering from the human condition. We all have the ability to suffer, have exposure, and vacillate between these conditions (I prefer this term rather than disorders) and it is my belief that we are each meant to work the best within the terms we have been dealt and take ownership and responsibility for our growth and our path forward.

A personality disorder should not be a shameful stigma as imposed on much of our western society today, but from my personal observation based on what I've seen in my clients and in my own personal relationships, individuals experiencing personality disorders are largely experiencing them as a result of their emotional body creating an imbalance of chemical response (fall out of the Svadhisthana/sacral) or possibly the influence of a dark entity. Essentially with effort, accountability, and dedication, these conditions of the human spirit can be eradicated or at least vastly reduced without indignity.

1. **Class A examples** - These 'disorders' are characterized within an individual's unconventional qualities and are classified by identifying an individual as eccentric.
    a. **Paranoid Personality Disorder** - results in distrust of peers and associates, and consistent suspicion of others. This condition often goes undiagnosed and people who experience this disorder typically live with it creating a pattern of self-sabotage or seductive patterns.

Individuals who suffer from this condition are common and believe that the people they are associated with or that they come in contact with create conflict either outwardly or intentionally perceiving that any and all remarks made are made maliciously when they could have been innocent. PPD sufferers tend to hold grudges even if the grudge began from an internal projection.

    b. **Schizoid Personality Disorder** - Lack of interest in social interaction or personal relationships. These individuals have a limited range of personal emotions and comes across as cold unavailable or distant. **This personality disorder is often misdiagnosed or manifests as the result of depression which is an imbalance of the Svadhisthana.**

    c. **Schizotypal Personality Disorder** - Schizotypal personalities have flat emotions, lack of social cues, lack of moral consciousness even though they could have been exposed to or have been raised with them.

2. **Class B examples** - These personality types are typically characterized by extreme unpredictable and an incompatibility personality:

    a. **Antisocial Personality Disorder** - Disregard for others needs or feelings. Persistent lying addiction to stealing, conning, repeated violation of the rights of others, impulsive behavior, irresponsible and lack of remorse for their behavior.

b. **Borderline Personality Disorder** - Impulsive and risky behavior, possibility of unstable and possessive intensity in relationships, frequent intense displays of anger, up and down moods as a result of internal stress, stress related paranoia.

c. **Histrionic Personality Disorder** - Attention seeking, extremely dramatic, seeks approval of others, influenced by others, tends to believe they are more important than others, and excessive concern with appearance as an outward perspective.

d. **Narcissistic Personality Disorder** - Believe they you are superior to others, failure to recognize or acknowledge other's needs and feelings, expectations of constant praise, take advantage of others, gaslights others, gossips and lies, envy others and believe that others envy them. Gaslighting is an abuser's method of manipulating another by making themselves the victim (their own associates tend to question the victim's sanity or sense of reality).

3. **Class C** - typically described as anxious and fearful:

**Avoidant Personality Disorder** - Sensitivities to criticism or rejection, low self-esteem, timid, and isolated.

a. **Dependent Personality Disorder** - Feelings of neediness or needs to be taken care of, submissive, fears disapproval, tolerates poor and abusive behavior.

b. **Obsessive-Compulsive Personality Disorder** - Extreme perfectionism, inability to let go of anything, rigid, and stubborn.

There are a few additional personality conditions and mental health challenges individuals can suffer from that can be correlated to broken down chakras or even passed on as a trait through genetics but can actually be reversed with accountability, dedication, a holistic mind-body-soul regimen, and professional care. Additional and popular personality conditions are, clinical depression, anxiety disorder, PTSD, bi-polar disorder, etc. These personality conditions are the most common among us and create imbalances in relationships and grow an individual's view of themselves in relation to the environment they commune with. It is generally believed that your personality is based on response to your external environment and it is shaped in each of our lives beginning in utero and fully formed by the time we are five-years old.

These personality traits can be harmful to the relationships they hold with others. **In those that do not suffer from these personality traits, our blockages that are created as a result of these traumatic relationships will continue to manifest in the relationships we attract if not healed. If you have a parent or sibling that has a personality disorder and has caused you unhealed strife, you will continue to replicate these relationships in others until you heal.** These personality traits can also be genetic, influenced by the personalities a person is exposed to and their experiences. These indifferences are largely the impact of trauma and having lack of stable emotional support. This is the truth about generational curses. As we might be aware, the state of humanity is largely toxic and because of this it is common to see many people in relationships attempting to reclaim their power in varying ways but doing so in an individualized effort rather than from a perspective of unified consciousness.

## HOW DO WE HELP?

*"Never make a permanent decision over temporary discomfort."*
*– Bishop T.D. Jakes.*

We cannot 'make' anyone change. Accountability of any personality's undesired behavior as a response mechanism to one's environment for the benefit of making a healthy contribution to society is key. Chances are, we know many people who fall under these categories. These diagnoses are largely misunderstood or not contextualized well. I believe the missing component is understanding the emotional body and unlocking blockages, but you cannot help anyone by aiding their recovery or by fixing broken relationships if they are not accountable and willing to take a step forward. There are circumstances where the outcome of a personality disorder is circumstantial and not something one has done to themselves intentionally. I see this a lot. We cannot blame so many today for turning out the way they did and deal with lack of resources and information available about what trauma really does to our emotional body, but once we are aware, we do have a choice.

I have found the most effective way to help an individual that has a personality disorder is a 1:1 reiki treatment. My sole efforts in life is to help anyone willing to eradicate these cycles.

## SOCIAL PSYCHOLOGY

Attachment Theory- Attachment theory is the bond between two people in various stages in relationships. It is the "lasting psychological connectedness between two people."- John Bowlby. Attachment begins in a state of infancy and continues throughout an individual's life.

## TREE OF LIFE AND THE MANIPURA

Imagine the solar system in relation to the tree of life. Ancient cultures all depict the tree of life within their codex's and hieroglyphics demonstrating that they had far more knowledge of the association to the meanings of life than we have been enabled to perceive today. As well as our Manipura, each produce a stream of energy omitting from the core of its energy source. For the sun, we relate this experience in terms of a solar flare. It is a large amount of radiation (energy). These solar flares that omit from the sun, our bodies also omit through our Manipura's as electromagnetic waves. This can be done through all of the chakras but is most prevalent here. Life on earth relies heavily on the solar energy transmitted from the sun to the earth and its electromagnetic waves (electromagnetic is defined exactly as described, it is the interrelation of the electric masculine currents with magnetic feminine currents).

Ultimately it is through the solar flares that unified consciousness and ascension are intended to raise the global vibration of the planet to a functioning fifth dimensional atmosphere. This will continue to enable individuals to feel and see these waves and further interpret how they are impacting our lives.

These new levels of consciousness will enable us all to have strong influences on human and animal health among all of the six living species. We will continue to break down the impacts of personality disorders, mental health conditions, physical ailments, and bring systemic abuse patterns to a close allowing pathway for new galactic generations to emerge from the circumstances our society currently offers.

Protons are essentially a measurable radiant source of energy. The photons we as individuals omit are housed within our Manipura. As Albert Einstein's theories and tests prove, no matter how much a beam of light is recorded and chased after, light/energy will always exceed you... So, if you are omitting trauma... that traumatic energy has exceeded you and permeating your future timelines. Full function of the Manipura is in fact what connects us to everything; all sources of energy and all of consciousness. The only thing that stops us from this connection is us, systemic abuse patterns, and the programming we have all been subjected to.

The Manipura further connects to our additional chakras and is what gives us our initial connection and interpretation to the spirit realms. Energy is constant and its manipulation is what has constructed the 'laws' that apply to 'time."

Time is another form of a fragmentation which we'll discuss in brief later. This study supports the conclusion that time doesn't really exist and it is a construct of the human species. This concept of time in the form of photons and particles of life are each translated to the tree of life. The Manipura is connected to the sephira #7 Netzach/Victory and #8 Hod/Glory.

## NETZACH/VICTORY

This sephira correlates to the number seven. Netzach's charge is a positive masculine charge. This sephira delivers direct energy channels to the ancillary chakras in the hips and further connects the meridian channels in the legs. Netzach represents instincts and emotion. The God aspect of this sephira is Jehovah Tzabaoth which is also known in other texts from my learnings as Jehovah Yaldabaoth, Tzabaoth, Sabboth, and Tsaba. Jehovah Tsaba, (as I am most familiar) Lord our warrior. This is the aspect/ energy that relieves us in mercy. Like a divine intervention. It is pure power and energy. The Arch Angel is Arch Angel Haniel whose responsibility is primarily over the emotion of joy, Universally, Netzach correlates to the planet Venus and is from the realm, angelic order of the gods with a little g.

## HOD/GLORY

This sephira is number eight. This is the sephira that holds a feminine magnetic charge. Hod/Glory is where intellectual powers are held and where the full activated power of the Netzach through Yesod come into light. Hod, takes the emotional charge created in Yesod, processed through Netzach and executes the energy into action form. This sephira has the most impact and potency to manifestation qualities. Law of attraction can be largely applied here. Full functioning Manipura, Svadhisthana, and Muladhara chakras will create the most fluid manifestations. Blocked or clouded chakras will manifest similar external qualities in our lives when we utilize these resources for manifestation purposes. The God aspect of this sephira is Elohim Tzabaoth or Jehovah Jireh which means the Lord our

Provider. What might God see so that he can provide for your life? Your realization of full manifestation ability lies within these qualities. The Arch Angel that correlates is Arch Angel Michael. The realm and angelic order are Ben Elohim, Emissaries of Light, or sons of God. This sephira is primarily associated to the planet Mercury.

## PATHS OF NETZACH AND HOD

Path 27 connects Netzach and Hod is consummated and associated to the orb of the sun which creates 'Excited Intelligence' or 'Natural Intelligence." It is through this path that meditation unlocks the power of the spirit and provides manifestation into the physical world.

After a review of all that's listed above, can you see how the Muladhara, Svadhisthana, and Manipura all have a cyclical play into the lives of us all? The Hermetic Principle that applies to the Manipura/solar plexus is the law of causation. Cause and effect are merely a result of events. **There is a relationship between everything that has gone before and all that follows**. There is no such thing as 'chance.'

# THE SUN IN CONNECTION TO THE MANIPURA

These electromagnetic waves are broken down into three categories as well connecting directly to the function of the electromagnetic grid that surrounds the earth. The waves are categorized as wavelength, frequency, and amplitude. **Wavelengths are the distance between the peaks**. Our bodies are also transmitting energy through manifestation into our environment and surroundings in number oscillations the waves produce within a second. The wavelength is the distance between the peaks, and I hypothesize that they further relate to the receptivity of the wave by the organism. The amplitude of these waves equals the height and depth or the waves.

Imagine for a second that through your Manipura, you receive and omit responses to this energy the same way that the sun transmits these electromagnetic waves to your own body. This process allows your soul to manifest and that is why it is so important to operate in your life with clear and free energetic portals within your emotional body. There are many great spiritual leaders and educators among us, such as one of my personal favorites from the perspective of energy waves, Aluna Ash from a spiritual aspect and my dear friend Michael Lazaro from a physical aspect. You can find him on YouTube and Patreon. Again, as above, so below.

## MERKABAH

The process of healing our traumas mirrors the flow of energy of the tree of life releasing our energy flows in an upward spherical form which also relays to the same orbit of our planet as it occurs in layers. Once our chakra ports are fully cleared and open, we then connect to our auric bodies creating a radiant state of being. Thereafter, once our auric fields are cleared, we will then have begun to operate within our galactic capabilities and activate our Merkabah, the light body that surrounds us, our full energetic connection to all that is. Once these chains of events have occurred healing/opening and balancing our chakras, and the kundalini is activated, subsequently our Merkabah activates. Our bodies are not the only fields of energy that hold Merkabah ports of energy, our earth does as well, and they can be accessed through the Merkabah that surrounds our auric fields.

Science describes these ports of energy as earth's navels. Back to the topic of photons, essentially, **activated Merkabah is the dynamic charge that is created when two opposing charges combine to create a stream of electromagnetic energy;** much like kundalini or orgasmic energy. An activated Merkabah can be described as being in a state of pure divine energy. The experience is like no other. I frequent this state of being and have been able to activate this state of being in others as well. Although all the chakras can be a port for the soul's astral experience, the Manipura is the largest port for the soul experience to astral travel. I move further and dare to further hypothesize that some forms of personality conditions and even autism is actually an individual who is stuck between frequencies and does not have the ability to maintain existence in one state or another creating what the world's professionals deem as dysfunction.

A healthy Merkabah can expand the body up to sixty feet in the best of sages. It holds the type of energy that creates a positive impact on its surroundings. The Bible describes this in the book of Ezekiel as the 'Chariots of Fire.' Ascended masters, in human form as well, such as Enoch, (whose books were removed from the Bible and who was Noah's grandfather) were able to use this energy force field for communication to higher realms, spirit, and allow interstellar travel. It is the full energetic manifestation of the union of the DNA (the tree of life), the emotional body, and our auric body. It is the Holy Trinity. You get the picture, I'm sure...

The Star Tetrahedron is the intersection of two perfect pyramids (triangle forms of energy flows) which create a third dimensional hexagram (We will discuss hexagrams in more detail when we discuss the heart chakra). It provides union, an alchemical process to fully realize manifestation and the process of the earth is largely accessed through the earth's energetic ports and the wonders of the world are located on most of the energy ports. It is believed that in these locations, the souls with activated Merkabah fields are able to access different dimensions and each of the 9+ historical temples known as the 'wonders of the world', each have a space dedicated to this aspect of the soul's ability to astral travel.

Astral travel is a master level topic as its base is vast but helping our clients to know that this is the ultimate state of human consciousness is important. The background of such is the understanding in our current experiences. All occurrences in our universe do in fact correlate to a collective conscious level and furthermore into each and every one of our individual lives.

## MERIDIANS

Our body's and the Earth's Meridians are an internal flow of energy throughout our bodies that respond to the energy of our environment that we receive through our Manipuras. It is the flow of "Qi" in our bodies and is the primary subject of Chinese medicine. There are approximately twelve primary meridian points and twenty companion meridian points. Our chakra ports send initial signals out to our meridians which further connect to our yin (magnetic feminine charge) and tang (electric masculine charge) organs. The currents of energy flow model the flow of blood through our body circulating from head to feet.

Chinese medicine teachings break our internal organs and systems down into two categories:

1. Yin:
    a. Heart (Hands)
    b. Liver
    c. Spleen
    d. Lungs
    e. Kidneys

2. Yang:
    a. Gallbladder
    b. Stomach
    c. Bladder
    d. Intestines

Why is your nervous system important and what does it actually do with your emotional body?

The nervous system is further connected to the Manipura. When our emotional bodies hold blockages or are overactive, the fall out of the Manipura impact the following functions:

- Sends messages received from the external environment to the brain.
- Connects the brain, neurons, nerves, and spinal cord.
- Involuntary messages and signals to the heart allowing blood flow, the lungs allowing breathing, and digestion through the intestines.
- Voluntary messages such as physical responses to our environment, words we choose to speak, decision making, etc.
- Processes our intake from our five senses (hearing, vision, taste, feeling, and smell)
- Connects functions of the heart chakra

CHAPTER SEVEN

# THE MANIPURA

OUR MANIPURA, OR solar plexus is the emotional link to our soul. It's our personal power. **A balanced solar plexus allows us to be assertive and display self-confidence**, our storehouse for manifestation, and our relationship to the environment we are in. **An imbalanced or blocked Manipura will demonstrate itself through excessive desire and need to project excessive control, overexertion of power, obsessive behavior, and an inability to let go of details, being manipulative, lack of purpose or ambition, etc.** The frequency of this chakra is often referred to as the miracle frequency and resonates sound waves at 528 HZ through 696 HZ and focuses on repairing the cells. The color that resonates with the solar plexus is yellow. Arch Angel Michael, Arch Angel Haniel, and other Arch Angel that helps maintain the Manipura functions is Arch Angel Uriel.

## TRAUMAS/BLOCKAGES INCLUDE:

Physical Abuse
Neglect
Blows to the Abdomen, stomach, kidneys, liver, or adrenal glands
Anxiety
Restlessness
Agitation
Fibromyalgia

Nausea/ sweating
Acid reflux
Diabetes
Fragmentations

Trauma causes an individual to begin to exist within a shell of existence. Our full capabilities cannot and will not be realized until we fully open up our emotional bodies. Some attribute healing, (as I once did as well) to be a highly functioning individual, but most times what we really do is stuff the trauma. When we do this instead of fully healing and opening, we end up manifesting disease. **Fragmentations are most often created through threshold or complex trauma and plays itself out into physical reality altering our state of being, creating an unknowing low-level consciousness, and undesired states of being.**

Fragmentation can be further defined as and is referred to in the clinical world as 'dissociation.' This is when the individual loses touch with reality and this act is the polarized function of astral travel. Many individuals today suffer from fragmentation, just as the result of living in a society which practices and follows programming tactics that the majority of our world follows today. **Fragmentation typically occurs for an individual who has already experienced trauma.**

## FRAGMENTATION/DISSOCIATIVE SYMPTOMS INCLUDE:

- Abnormal changes in mood
- Drama/ Creating Chaotic Environments
- Lack of coping resources
- Newly Developed Personality Disorder
- Oppositional Defiance
- Personality change
- Social Abnormalities

## ENTITY/SPIRIT POSSESSIONS

Unfortunately, we do have to go there. There is a lot of fear and mysticism that surrounds this topic, especially within western culture, but this is a subject matter I am seeing time and time again with several of my clients. This is, among many revered healing subjects, the primary communicated healing ability of Yeshua, Jesus Christ, as so many of us believe in.

Jesus demonstrated the act of removing spirit possessions many times within the Bible. He's not the only one though…it is a common practice among many religions and walks of life although it has become a cache subject. Jesus was not only attempting to teach us to be good Christ Conscious human beings, He was showing us that we have the ability to remove entity attachments but for fear, dogma, and programming, our society does not embrace this ideology.

Treatment of this subject has actually inadvertently become a specialty of mine within the last few years. On my journey as an energy healing practitioner, I was not looking to for the intention to do this, but have been called to, so I embrace it. I am not afraid of it, and I am no longer fearful of how people respond to it as I do not care what the external world thinks of this healing ability. And there are many of us who can and do. There are several individuals who practice the art of hands-on energetic healing in this way should the need arise.

When you think about the ability to relieve this type of trauma is actually pretty cool and is a blessing nonetheless of Source and is the utmost use of universal energy as science describes. But, let's discuss what we need to know about this subject in relation to trauma recovery. Enoch (who is now Arch Angel Metatron) and many other ancient texts, also fully describe how demonic entities and entities of darkness have come about within several writings and teachings. The books of Enoch were once intact in the Bible and have since been removed. They have been translated and can be purchased as well. Its contents are in fact still intact in the Dead Sea Scrolls which is the oldest known version of the Bible; although many scholars and researchers will conclude that the Bible is actually a loose version of the Emerald Tablets or the Sumerian Texts...that, however, is another story for another time.

These entities will come as you enlighten. An entity is a non-physical energetic being that can attach itself to a host to harness the energy it needs to manifest its unfulfilled desires or the desires the entity was directed through dark magic to obstruct on an individual. The entity controls the 'host' body which leads to vast differences in the being's behavior, relationships, or ability to function properly in life. Unfortunately, as a result of living within a fear-based society, western culture has not publicly advanced its practices to appropriately identify these individuals. Some people, no matter what level of exposure they've had to it, act like it doesn't exist which actually encourages entities to rage on. The ignorance is what is keeping them going. It doesn't work the other way around like so many believe. These entities largely attach themselves to the human spirit through the Manipura, the solar plexus.

There are some beautiful souls that believe that energy healing of the emotional body, as a result of a dogmatic belief system, believe that this work, unlocking the emotional body, is how entities are able to connect to us. Nothing could be farther from true. Entities actually seduce and use their hosts through blockages, unresolved or stuffed traumas, and underbalanced chakras draining the energy of the person. When our energy is free and flowing, especially if we are operating from our light bodies, Christ consciousness, this energy creates a force field or a shield of protection around us which is truly how we protect our energy, not the other way around. As a master practitioner, I have released entities time and time again.

Entities can be induced by others and are attracted to the wounds of the human soul. Including the wounds that have been passed down through etheric imprinting from generation to generation. Some individuals attract an entity from a state of loneliness or codependency. Some people go an entire lifetime with an entity attachment and never even know. Typically, these entities are and become dark in nature because it passed on itself with unresolved traumas.

**The most common emotional states an entity attaches itself to is:**

- Altered states of consciousness (hypnosis, prescribed medication, misguided meditations)
- Emotional Shock
- Etc.
- Grief
- Heavy drug and alcohol use
- Over exposure to death
- Personality Disorders and the subsequent behaviors
- Psychic Abilities (mediumship, etc.)
- Recipient of dark magic

These entities can and may cause severe fatigue; physical illness; increases psychic or paranormal receptivity; addictive behaviors; intensified feelings and responses in rage, grief, violence, fear, or anything including approaching life in general, a topic, or an individual; drastically altering one's self esteem and self-care practices; and/or alters one's interpersonal relationships with loved ones turning these emotions to the opposing end of the emotion usually to hate, envy, jealousy, spite, and retaliation.

Essentially, the 'host' body takes on the energy and personality traits of the entity and will oppose anything or anyone that can alter its influence over the host. Seducing and possessing entities also know when to attach themselves and when to detach from an individual. Some entities are not demonic in nature, but if it possesses another's body in a way that alters one's emotions and state of being or worse, absolute dark in nature. **It is important for us to have the highest level of protection and to do this we need to heal our emotional bodies.**

More advanced demonic entities will not only possess a host, it will also create an overtangle network. This overtangle (which we will discuss at length when we review the functions of the crown chakra) of individuals, will create a community of individuals that impact every living being around the subject host. The entity will seduce its subjects into the desires or will of the entity altering the state of being, interactions, and understanding of the overtangle which it controls. The only way to help avoid a demonic possession or overtangle influence is not just knowledge, it is through the active focus or clear emotional bodies, prayer, and sufficient connection to our spiritual light, teams of light and holy spirit. If an individual is allowing a blockage to occur or is living a life based on fear or a lie or holding on to a trauma, this individual is subject to direct possession or impact of an overtangle of negative influence. Entities can also use anything around you.

I have not personally had a spirit or entity possession and because I have not personally experienced this, I do not have a personal testimony for this specific topic although I've been fully exposed to them, but I will share a testimony about how another scenario opened my Manipura. These possessions happen more than they are acknowledged and can be seen throughout space and universal elements as well. This is the reason that so many never experience the power of a fully functioning Manipura and do not exceed the Svadhisthana, and sacral chakra functions.

I will however ask you to be open and ponder this... because of the close association of the signs of entity possession and the close association of altered character traits of personality disorders and mental illnesses, could it be that sometimes these altered states of consciousness or personality could additionally arise as the result of an entity possession?...

## HEALING RESOURCES

- Sound Healing (Entities, especially, do not like music or higher frequencies. This is one of the reasons I always have music playing.)
- Verbal Affirmations
- Ask for assistance from God, the universe, or spirit guides
- Quartz (smoky or clear), selenite, black obsidian, black tourmaline, or jet crystals.

## PERSONAL TESTIMONY

*When I was 6 years old, I lived in Washington D.C. I loved every single last bit of living in D.C. I was a happy kid there. I was nourished in every way possible and fully encouraged to be who I am in every way possible. I was given strategies to accept myself fully and given every single opportunity possible to share my gifts. I had options. MANY options. I lived in D.C. with my great grandmother Irene Nickerson Laney. At night, usually right around my bedtime, she would carry me out to the car in my pajamas and a blanket, buckle me into the back seat and then drive around the city. But while we were driving, we took adventures. We would drive through the capitol, North West D.C., and the suburbs surrounding D.C. in Virginia and Maryland.*

She took me through so many neighborhoods and this is where my love for home design began. We drove through the most beautiful neighborhoods. Not to mention, I thought (and still do) that my Grandma's neighborhood was amazing. It certainly was amazing to live in and grow up in! Her neighbors were also all amazing people. The thing I loved the most about D.C. was the rain. In D.C. the rain is usually very heavy with big rain drops. We used to play in the rain and dance in the rain all the time. I still play in the rain to this day. This is where my whole life began, especially my love of nature. We truly do gain most of the personality by the time we are five-years old, the rest of our time is spent responding to our environment, but boy was I lucky. And I'm grateful. Who I am today is mostly because of who she was. And wow, she was pretty amazing!

Once, after a long and wet rainy afternoon, I couldn't wait to get outside. That was my favorite moment in nature. It still is. I went outside and no one from the neighborhood kids were out yet. So instead of going and ringing all the doorbells of my friends so they would come outside (I used to always get all the kids out at the same time. I loved having everyone together. I went from house to house asking for every single kid in the neighborhood to come outside together. We used to be a pretty large group of kids!!) I get happy just thinking about those days! Anyhow, I digressed, I decided to stay alone that day... I went outside and stood with just my toes in the sunshine while standing under a tree in front of my grandmother's house; whose branches were so low and full it was like standing under a big umbrella.

It was amazing! On this particular day in late August, a few weeks just before I would begin first grade, the clouds broke, *and the sun shined through and hit me as I stood under this tree directly from my toes and worked its way up my body. I felt the warmth of the sun's rays from my toes all the way to the crown of my head as the clouds parted and the sun's light emanated over me...it was in that moment that I fully realized that God... was present in this moment and that our sun, had something to do with God. I knew in that moment that we and everything on this planet are connected. I opened my eyes and stared directly into the sunlight, and my internal knowing was forever changed after that moment.*

*I stood there in shock. I can still feel exactly how I felt at that moment. I turned around and looked beyond my grandmother's front yard, through the windows, and all the plants in her solarium on the sun porch at my great grandmother's house and right into my great grandmother's eyes and she nodded very slowly to me and smirked at me. I knew she knew I had just experienced something amazing. With her silent encouragement, I turned back around and began my first meditation with nature.... It opened my Manipura.*

## SPIRITUAL GIFTS

The gift associated with the Manipura is the gift of manifestation. Manifest to be defined at best, is the ability to believe deeply within your spirit. It is the essence of unwavering faith from the essence of the origin to fruition. We are each manifesting at every moment of each of our existence. With a clear root and sacral chakra, the solar plexus allows us to be in alignment with our desires wants and needs. We will manifest in both the positive and negative aspects of life. **When you have**

**blockages, your world will reflect that back to you through every encounter you have.** When you are functioning freely, your world will be like an oyster in the palm of your hand. You will operate freely on your life and all that you are meant to be in alignment with when you came into this 'physical form' will be without resistance.

## CLAIRCOGNIZANCE

Claircognizance is the clear unwavering knowing of absolute truth without the use of the other senses. **It is the internal download that needs no interpretation.** Claircognizance is radically different from clairempathy or clairsentience however much like the use of these other gifts, if chakras are overstimulated this knowing can lead into knowing that is unbalanced and breaks boundaries. It is important that we always remember just because we may 'know' through our claircognizance, there are some things we are not meant to know.

CHAPTER EIGHT

# THE ANAHATA

**S**O FAR ON our journey, we have covered the unconscious state of being, how our emotional body ties into our functioning mind, and are now venturing into our conscious 'I am me' state of being. The Anahata is the 'gateway' to higher levels of consciousness.

The Anahata is considered a bridge and projects itself as your actual third dimensional reality. The Anahata is the center of all that is within our current world and is the projection for our external relationships. The Anahata with its ties to the body's heart, is our second brain. Many studies show that the brain is the most crucial organism, I disagree. **I believe the heart is the most crucial organism and intellectual muscle/organ of the human body.**

Just imagine, we can still live without a full functional brain, or mental intelligence, or our intestines our intuitive intelligence, but we cannot live without a functioning heart. Our soul can still be tied to our physical bodies at those other points. But with heart failure and without medical support to revive the heart's functionality we cannot live. As we know, in western culture and most of the dominant cultures we are encouraged to operate at an unconscious root level. Ideally, in helping to cultivate a 5th dimensional level of consciousness, we are encouraging humanity to live from the Anahata, a state of unconditional love and a constant compassion for our fellow human species, and all of the additional six living species. We are currently being encouraged to become more balanced within our relationship to the animal kingdom and our levels of consciousness will continue to grow.

# THE TREE OF LIFE AND THE ANAHATA

It is here through our Anahata, our heart chakra, that all of mankind is being encouraged to evolve. Our ancestors and ancient civilizations once fully functioned within this capacity of being and as a result, we held states of communal relationships and lived in a constant state of compassion. Because of our conditioning, full functioning of the heart space is hard to maintain. Ancient civilizations knew that compassion was the reason for humankind and conducted all that they did based on these principals. We are being encouraged to encompass all that we have been enabled to learn throughout modern history and once again lead us back to this emotional state.

The sephira associated to the Anahata is the sephira Tiphareth/Beauty. This sephira is number six on the tree of life and represents unconditional love. Before we delve into particulars, we can take a look at varying states of consciousness in many popular idols that we have become familiar with today. Lord Yeshua Ben Yosef (Jesus Christ), Lord Buddha, Paramahansa Yogananda, Dr. Mikao Usui, Lord Krishna, Egyptian God Osiris, Dr. Martin Luther King, and so many more, all Mastered the art of the function of the Anahata and this very compassionate based teaching was each of their lessons to their eager students. Each of their students who learn to function, without judgement or the presence of dogma, were able to attain life at this level of vibration and have each taught of the body's functions as a 'temple.'

Tiphareth/Beauty creates the energy of Chesod and Geburah which we will discuss when we discuss the throat chakra. The God name of this sephira is Jehovah Aloah Va Daath or Jehovah Shalom which means peace. Shalom is the stem of the word shalom which stands for the wholeness, a complete emotional state of reciprocity, the absence of conflict.

> *"Blessed are the peacemakers, for they shall be called the sons of God"*
> *– Matthew 5:9*

Tiphareth is where we begin to attain Christ Consciousness (this is not a term that is strictly tied to Christianity, it is merely a level of consciousness). The Arch Angel of this sephira/emotional body is Arch Angel Raphael and the realm is the realm of the Malachim and Royalty. Tiphareth is also identified by the sun as a result of the flow of the Manipura, the river of life, and the alchemical process of the creation of gold.

Tiphareth initiates the second trinity on the tree of life and energy flow in our emotional body. The purpose of the Tiphareth and the Anahata is transmutation of the third dimensional consciousness into a Divine state, that of the 5th dimension.

The paths that correlate to the Tiphareth are paths 24, 25, and 26. Path 24- Connects Tiphareth and Netzach (Anahata and Manipura/solar plexus). The path of created/ manifested relationships 'Imaginative Intelligence.' This is the path where we see 'like attracts like' into physical reality. Path 25- Connects Tiphareth and Yesod (Anahata and Svadhisthana/sacral chakra). 'Intelligence of Probation/Tentative.'

In life we are faced with many challenges and tests. This path is where those tests occur and our succession of them depends on whether or not we create karma and repeat a cycle or proceed forward within our energetic flows.

Path 26- Tiphareth and Hod (Anahata and Manipura/solar plexus) 'Renovating Intelligence' tied closely to the process of transmutation/alchemy as it correlates to Source energy by being renewed in our creation.

The Hermetic Principle and universal law that correlates to the Tiphareth/Beauty is 'Mental Transmutation.' Transmutation is a term that applies to the mental art through a fully functioning Anahata of changing metals into gold...mental Transmutation is the art of transforming mental forms into another...bringing balance to the pendulum swing. A balanced state between love and hate but allowing a full flow of love energy. It is from our heart, the Anahata that we will see real and effective change in the world and causing impact to the universal flow. The universe itself is a 'Mental Plane' and the functions of the Anahata are very distinctly tied to the plane of air and ether. It is the effect of the cause as produced with a freely flowing Manipura/solar plexus.

# ANAHATA/HEART CHAKRA

## WHAT IS YOGA?

Before our souls incarnate within our physical temples, we are one, blended with infinite light. Descending into these vessels from our energetic form from the flower of life structure we are each initiated from our souls are broken down into three distinct 'degrees.' According to the Kabbalah the process of life and death itself is called Aleph and the flow of the energy will fall into three categories throughout our lives.

I believe that these aspects can be attained over varying incarnations into physicality but can also be attained within one life cycle. The first as depicted within the Kabbalah is called **Neshamah, which is the highest state of consciousness identified with sephira Kether and the Sahasrara/crown chakra**. It is the state where one acquires a state of Dharma and begins a whole new cycle of self-awareness, knowledge, and relation to one's environment. **Neshamah is the cultivation of all that we are created to be**. It is the yin and yang and full balance. This cycle is related to the individual aspects of the soul.

The second 'degree' of the soul is Ruach. It is the heart, Tiphareth and Anahata/heart chakra flowing through the Yesod/sacral chakra. This cycle is tied to the process of karma and where relationships are born. These cycles being tied to karma are shown through our relationship patterns. These are where the lessons we, each as souls are meant to learn through our communal relationships to others. Our conscious mind is a result of the unconscious state we have created either knowingly or unknowingly. The phrase that we are a product of our environment is true until we know how to transmute those circumstances to better suited conditions; we are meant to live within each of our lives.

It is here where the law of attraction begins again, either knowingly or unknowingly. The last 'degree' or phase of the soul is called and is related to Qliphoth and can be tied to our innate internal struggle of good and evil and is tied to the will of the individual. It is tied to the judgements derived of unity and purity. **This aspect of our soul experience is tied to trauma, our dark night of the soul, our valley in the shadow of death.**

**This is where we see humanity at large today, but we are each required to have these experiences to fulfil our soul growth, destiny, and purpose.**

**Yoga is in fact the scientific process of uniting the individual soul with the cosmic spirit. It is in fact a union**. Yoga is a philosophical principle that combines mind, body, and spirit mirroring the aspects of the three pillars of the tree of life. Yoga was originated as one from the six orthodox philosophies of the Hindu faith.

There has been very little public and scientific research conducted at this point to the manifestation of the reality of the subconscious mind. The subconscious links have been made within the practice of yoga and the teachings, practices, and systems that have come of the result of the primary Samkhya principles. The universe and spirit are represented in all of its works and asanas (poses).

Yoga is the process that allows man to discover the light and divinity within. Yoga itself will produce what has been referred to as 'Yogi-Christ.' Yoga is not a sport or activity it is an actual physical science. It is the process of scientifically exercising emotional balance and mental control. The paths of yoga are correlated to the four paths the soul is intended to follow as bestowed in the tree of life soul 'degrees'; including the process of life and death as we each experience these phenomenons in varying smaller iterations throughout our lives. Most practitioners specialize in one area of practice, others blend a combination. I've further related the four paths to our general soul experiences as categorized within our soul paths as related to the tree of life.

## THE FOUR PATHS ARE:

1. Raja Yoga- This is the path of self-discipline. 'Drama' (defined by me as the process of life and death, birth and rebirth)
2. Jnana Yoga- This is the path of knowledge and self-realization. 'Trauma'
3. Bhakti Yoga- This is the path that leads to spiritual enlightenment. 'Karma'
4. Karma Marga Yoga- This is the path of action into unity consciousness. 'Dharma.'

Because the Anahata is associated to the element of air, all elements are fully supported within the function and again further create a trinity in the state of being within our emotional body. The Anahata is associated to the sounds of the celestial realm, which creates the utmost balance, calmness, and serenity. Yoga essentially ties these qualities together. Yoga is an integral part of soul growth; yoga was once practiced widely by the masses but has now been construed as 'mythical' in essence. Have you ever had a yoga session that left you feeling exceptional? This is why... The Western culture has largely created a yoga culture based on physical well-being only removing the spiritual intent and nature behind the practice attributing the source to a top forty pop culture, but nonetheless, any exposure to the yogi's experience is an asset to the soul's experience.

Your body is a temple. We will discuss more about the functionalities of physical temples in relation to your body in later context, but as our energetic system is tied to our emotional body, it is also physically connected to the functions of our spine. **Your entire body is a giant antenna and the practice of yoga is a pathway for those energy channels to be in tune and each asana is designed to help us keep our spiritual and emotional ailment.** Is yoga for everyone...yes! It is the pathway forward and no matter where you are physically, yoga always meets you where you are.

## POPULAR YOGA PRACTICES ARE:

1. Hatha Yoga- Hatha Yoga is for beginners and focuses on breathing, meditation, and postures. It is good for all levels because it is typically slow in nature.
2. Iyengar Yoga- provides an emphasis on detail, builds strength, and mobility.
3. Kundalini Yoga- influenced by Shaktism and Tantra combines mantras, tantra, and meditation.
4. Bikram Yoga-90 minutes and only works based on 26-postures and only two breathing exercises.
5. Sivananda Saraswati- spiritual yoga.
6. Yin Yoga- Slow paced asanas held for longer periods of time. Advanced practitioners hold positions for five minutes or more creating the most impact. Day Seven yoga practices and teaches principles of this yoga practice.

If you are interested and are so led to learn more about these types of yoga practices please visit our website here: https://www.daysevenwellnesscenter.com/shop

CHAPTER NINE

# SHAMBALA

**B**EFORE WE LOOK into Shambhala, let's take a trip down memory lane with grammar review and look at the definitions of a few specific terms for respectful debate and for the sake of the naysayers.

- Noun- A noun is used to identify a class of people, place, or thing.
- Adjective- is a word or a phrase that is added to a description that names an attribute of a person, place, or thing.

*Can we agree for a moment that a noun is the 'truth' of identity? It is a fact about a characteristic? For example, I am an African American Woman- These titles are each a noun. Let's further break down the statement, "I am 'enlightened.'" The term enlightened is an adjective that describes my current state of emotional awareness...let's further review the following definitions along the means of the definitions written above.

- Folktale- Is a noun that is carried through traditions by word of mouth. Essentially, we are made aware that because this term is classified by the characteristics of a noun, a folktale can absolutely be taken as truth.

- Mythical- Mythical actually means 'occurring in and characteristic of myths or folktales.' Its synonyms are "legendary, mythological, fabulous, storybook, and more.' Traditional definitions move forward to describe mythical as 'idealized especially when referenced to the past.

Globally we have been led to believe that mythical is not pure in nature. I've come to learn that most of what is deemed mythical has some substantiating evidence in actuality at some point in the history of mankind. Please take of that what you will and hold the truth you believe, but please also keep in mind we have been misled for quite a long time so that we can be oppressed and operate at the will of others to achieve a will that is outside of our own. **I have always been hungry for spiritual knowledge**. Many years ago, during my quest to understand varying Aboriginal teachings and cultures, after the research of many Aboriginal cultures I landed at the knowledge of Shambala.

Essentially, Shambala is an actual civilization that already operates solely from the heart space, the higher levels of consciousness and subconscious and has existed for thousands and thousands of years. They are in fact the ideal civilization and what we would each strive to live like in an ideal world. But that world is coming to a community near you soon as we ascend to a $5^{th}$ dimensional level of consciousness.

This civilization has operated largely in secret but has opened its way and practices to the world at large as we gear up to live completely conscious lives in a state of unity and Christ consciousness. One of the most profound references to this civilization is the Marvel movie, 'Black Panther' which depicts the community of Wakanda as an advanced civilization operating in varying ways beyond the means of the modern world. Wakanda is in fact based on the truth in the Shambala culture.

As the earth changes, the base of Shambala changes location with the earth's vibrational shift. But through my personal guidance it was revealed to me that through changing hands of leadership of all kinds, Shambala will eventually once again become a state of existence for all. The Black Panther movie was a wonderful introduction of the topic and way of life. I rejoiced at the works of Black Panther. The other great resource about this knowledge is from author James Redfield, who is one of the most successful authors of all time with the writings of the world renown 'The Celestine Prophecies' which spent three-years straight on the New York Times best seller list. James Redfield's writings reflect tales and stories of his own spiritual journeys and 'The Secret of Shambala' is one of them. I'd recommend you read his books in succession if you are into that and are newly awakened.

Sharing this knowledge of this state of being within the topic of the Anahata and related to the topic of trauma is important because how do you know where you're going if you don't know where you come from? Our healing is pivotal in the evolution of mankind. The only way to get here and to get the actual call to Shambala, is through the process of healing. I personally have been called to help bring us to this state of Shambala here within physical awareness and being, through teaching and helping souls navigate the realms of their traumas, break the grips of systemic abuse patterns by recognizing the benefits in the lessons of their most challenging moments, how these moments apply to our lives overall, and understanding the pathway forward.

The basis of the Shambala kingdom and communities are the inner rungs the outer rungs and the temples. This third dimensional reality of this current civilization does in fact still exist and within this kingdom. The realities within this realm of existence is a combination of visual, spiritual, and physical reality. Shambala is a traveling civilization and follows the paths of the natural flow of energy within the earth. The earth's kundalini. Yes, the earth has kundalini too. It has been said that this civilization has occupied communities in Africa, Tibet, and is now believed to be in Costa Rica as well. In the outer rungs are the physical positioning of the community that has a forcefield of energy tightly woven so that only individuals with the appropriate level of frequency can enter. The inner rungs I'll describe as those with our own inner properties as manifestation. Because the citizens of the Shambala culture operate at higher frequencies most of their physical reality is created by the intangible energetic sources as not to hold up space but will operate for as long as the energy is needed. **The technology Shambala's citizens have access to is that in which we would consider sci-fi in nature. But it's very real.** The temples are the places of communal worship where the elders commune with angels and maintain deep meditative states and work together to send awareness, healing energy, and peace to all of mankind all over the world. What a state of human existence we are helping to usher in by healing our own traumas and in turn helping to repair the wounds of our fellow mankind and ultimately leading to as much of creation as possible. What a beautiful vision for our futures.

## HEXAGRAMS

In sacred geometry, there is a system that is present in lifeforms that are functioning in conscious capacity called hexagram. A hexagram is an energetic system of two interloping trinities of energy flow. Hexa = six; which is equivalent to the Tiphareth sephira that is in representation of beauty and unconditional love. The star of David is a popular image that correlates to the purpose. The hexagram is the symbol of the combination of the four elements Fire, Air, Water, and Earth. And further correlate to our internal emotional energy flows.

According to Hermetic Principles, the energy flow of the hexagram is the course of the traditional seven planets and further breaks down the sephiroth's on the tree of life. When in perfect balance and harmony, our emotional body holds an energetic flow in succinct pattern of a hexagram of energy between our chakra systems creating the conscious state of awareness.

## HEXAGRAM

# THE ANAHATA AND THE BODY SYSTEMS

Being comprised of a complex hexagram energy flow, the functions of the heart are quite complex and just as the energetic flow overlaps, so do the functions in which the Anahata contribute to. The body systems that are associated to the Anahata are the circulatory and muscular systems.

The circulatory/Cardiovascular System transports blood throughout our body. This blood flow runs concurrently with the energy flow of our meridian flows from the solar plexus. The circulatory system transports nutrients and oxygen to the blood and operate the heart, blood vessels, kidneys, and lungs. Because your heart is also a muscle and not an organ, it is also tied to the muscular system and is one of the hardest working muscles within our bodies aside from our brains. Our muscular system gives our bodies movement, works with our internal organs, and require oxygen and blood flow for energy.

## BREATH WORK

A basic principle of life within these physical bodies is breath itself. With each breath we take, we are taking in union with the universe and all of life's creation as we all are intertwined and have varying aspects of our energetic flows that work simultaneously within the six major kingdoms of consciousness. The primordial sound within the Anahata is 'OM.' This is believed to be the actual sound your heart makes. One of the many ways the human lifespan has been shortened and gotten stuck in the death and rebirth cycles within the earthly existence, is through the lost art of breathing. In ancient civilizations, even in depiction of Biblical stories, humans lived for hundreds and thousands of years and proper breath work is one of the reasons why.

There are many ways to breathe and pull energy into our bodies, aside from yogi's and masters of all kinds of arts; synchronized swimmers also utilize some of these techniques, but for now we will go over the breath work that will help fully open up your chakras and internal energy flows helping you to breathe deeper and in appropriate fashion. These are basic techniques; as an exercise, try these breathing techniques one at a time for a few days each and see how your body responds. It is remarkable the improvements you'll experience. Working these practices into a daily meditation routine makes an incredibly healthy contribution to everything we do and has an extraordinary impact on our personal and interpersonal relationships.

1. **Breath Retention aka Kumbha** - Sitting in a Kumbhaka Pranayama (comfortable sitting posture or crisscross applesauce) This inhale is called Antara, which is where you inhale into your heart space and pull your ribs into your expanded lungs. The exhale, Bahya is done in the opposite way. The goal is to be able to increase holding your breath to be able to say 'OM' slowly up to three times in each succession.

2. **Channel Cleaning Breath** - Cleans and purifies. Sitting comfortably and combining Mrigi Mudra which is the index finger connected to the thumb. Breathe deeply 3-5 times before combining chan-

nel work. Alternate breath channels from right to left nostril using ring finger and little finger for the left nostril and thumb for the right nostril. I find this breathing technique to be a great way to distinguish an emotion of anger and bring a sense of calmness. This is also a great breathing technique to start each day with as soon as you wake up.

3. **Conqueror Breath** - This breath work can be done while sitting comfortably or done in any asana. Inhale slowly with your nose and exhale slowly with your mouth open making a slight hissing noise. This breath work can be done to transmute energy as well if you are experiencing negative emotions in any way. This breathing technique should be done initially for 5-10 minutes and eventually advanced to 10-15 minutes.

4. **Deer Seal** - With a fisted hand, extend ring and pinky fingers (either hand works) and sitting in a comfortable position keeping your head and shoulders in equal and stable alignment. Keeping your elbow loosely tucked into your side, alternating grip back and forth between closing the right and left nostril breath in deeply through one nostril while the other is held closed with your pinky and ring finger release and switch nostrils on the exhale. Repeat 2-3 times and then breathe deeply and normally 2-3 times. Do another session/rep. I find that this technique helps with focus through breathing deeply into the belly creating balance and flow, belly/sacral, area

and will sharpen focus on a task once completed. This is a great way to begin a yoga lesson.

5. **Lion Pose** - Lion's breath pulls circulation from the lower organs and chakras and creates renewed flow and circulation to the third eye. For your inhale you will keep your palms and fingers open and flat against the knees or a solid surface. Keep your eyes closed while taking a deep breath in to the solar plexus area and on the exhale open the eyes, rolling your eyes upward while simultaneously exhaling through sticking the tongue out of the mouth as far as you can and release and push your breathe out of the solar plexus area with a long haaaa sound while keeping your palms and fingers stretched.

6. **Root Bond** - This breathe work should always be guided and with a partner. Sit or lay in a comfortable position. To begin, you start by squeezing or pulling tension into your pelvic and root area. With each hand push your hips as if you were pushing them to join each other and simultaneously begin your inhale. Pulling your breath as deep as you can into your root area on the exhale release and relax releasing all of the air from your body. While this a Muladhara/root centered breath technique, it will awaken the energy flow throughout your spine creating a consistent flow of energy. This is a great breathing technique to do in partnership prior to going to bed or to end a group yoga session.

7. **Skull Shining Breath** - One of my favorite breathing techniques. This is the technique that will ultimately lead to crown chakra breathing which is also referred to as life source breathing. (You may eventually breath through each of your chakra energy ports, your skin, your hands and feet, and your ears. I do it daily, but it takes a lot of mastery.) Inhaling slowly and deeply, you retain the breath for about five seconds, forcefully breath out again through your nose but push the breath up through your skull which will exhale the breath through your crown. This is the breath that creates the halo some see within the auric field of another. Repeat this for about 25-30 rounds.

8. **Bonus Breath Technique** Single Nostril Breath- This is typically a practice of Hatha yoga but can be attributed to helping cure a multitude of diseases. 'Ha' stands for happiness and 'Tha' stands for health. This is another technique that can be tied to sacral and throat chakras and all organs impacted within these regions. Use your thumb to alternate channeled breathing while breathing in the warmth of the sun, positive charges and exhale the cool of the moon, magnetic charges. I find this breath technique works best while preparing for prayer or manifestation and is a great technique to practice while in nature.

I hope you've reviewed this with an objective in mind because with our breath alone, so much can be accomplished. If and before your reject this knowledge, or if you are skeptical because of the detail I've shared, or if you are down for the count... ask yourself this question...why would you be encouraged to forget the proper and traditional ways to breathe?

Visit our YouTube channel, Day Seven Wellness here: http://bit.ly/dayseven-center-youtube for more information and guidance on breathing techniques and to help relieve specific areas of day to day tensions and traumas.

CHAPTER TEN

# THE ANAHATA

**THE ANAHATA IS** the chakra that is the source of our compassion and unconditional love vibration. During this time of the great ascension process it is the goal to relieve the entire world, including Gaia of its traumas so that we can function freely within our heart space. The possibility to vacillate between heart and root space is possible as they are connected channels, but if we are dealing with traumas and experiencing energies of anything other than unconditional love for ourselves and all there is, we are not fully functioning from our heart space. But this is the ultimate goal. We see these blockages and overactivity in each of our everyday lives with broken homes and in dysfunctional relationships. The color that correlates Anahata is green, the frequency is 639 HZ- 741 HZ. The Arch Angel is Arch Angel Raphael and its tied to the Intuitive Astral Body in our auric field.

## THE ANAHATA MAINTAINS FUNCTIONS OF:

- Bronchial Tubes
- Diaphragm
- Heart and the circulatory system
- Immune System
- Lungs
- Skin, Shoulders, Arms, and Hands

- Thymus Gland
- Upper Back

**At this point in humanity, there is no individual that has not experienced trauma and dysfunction. And that's okay. It has all happened to allow each of us the soul growth we needed to make the most impact on our lives and push us to pursue heart space unity consciousness.** A balanced and functioning Anahata will enable us to live lives full of compassion for all that is, peaceful experiences, humanitarian based efforts, reciprocity in relationships, and operating from this space will change the innate sexual culture and desire from operating sexually from a root space to understanding the importance to wait for the energy exchange with the right partner. **We are meant to give open and freely without expectation but have a natural exchange within a reciprocity-based civilization.** Living consciously from the heart space will not allow us to judge another for where they are on their journey in any way, instead providing space and energy to allow our neighbors to grow.

The dysfunctions and misappropriation of the use of the heart and Anahata are so common among us, it has many people projecting behaviors and rejected love looking at loving exchanges as terms of disrespect and at some level not identifying them for the trueness of what they are. It is okay to love everything and to express that love to everything and everyone. The program this generation and many before us have been faced with is the direct manipulation of the Anahata energy. Your body is your temple. We will discuss the temples use in later chapters but don't forget that. Anahata blockages or over activity will also cause extreme lack of trust and extreme narcissism in many cases. As we can see Narcissism as a contentious point in the wave of love frequency with hate being the polar opposite.

**Physical dysfunctions, illness, and disease of the Anahata will show themselves in heart disorders, lung disorders, breast disorders, thymus/thyroid hypo (under) activity/hyper (over) activity, arms, asthma, circulation problems, immune system deficiency, shoulder blade tension.**

# WHAT TRAUMAS CAUSE THESE AILMENTS FROM AN EMOTIONAL PERSPECTIVE?

1. Abandonment
2. Abuse and blockages of the lower chakras
3. Addictions
4. Betrayal
5. Death and grief
6. Divorce and breakups
7. Negative criticism
8. Rejection of all kinds
9. Sexual and physical abuse
10. Shaming
11. Verbal abuse

# THE HANDS AND THE ANAHATA

Popular themes of healing topics related to the Anahata are self-discovery, clearing patterns of codependency, inner child healing, and breath work to boost immune system functions and increase energy flow. **The Anahata as a central point of energy also controls our hands were, we have fourteen additional chakras! This is why the power of healing lies within our hands.** The freer and clear you are emotionally, the more of an innate healer you will become through touch. Adding resources and extended knowledge and techniques (such as reiki, yoga, and other healing modalities to move energy flows) to this area are the most impactful levels of healing. For the chakras in your hands, there are one in the middle of each palm, one in the start of each wrist, and one in each of our fingers and thumbs. **Our hands are the source of energy for the entire world.** Healing energy constantly passes through our hands with the right hand being predominant in giving and the left hand in receiving. I believe in this fashion more than the dominant hand theory as energy relates to the positive and magnetic or male and female aspects within each of us.

Practice…activating the energy in your hands is actually important and will increase your circulation. As a result of increased circulation, you'll have a healthier immune system, younger looking skin, and healthier relationships. Varying types of arthritis can be remedied by utilizing these methods as well. I'd recommend doing this when you are entering intimate circumstances such as family gatherings, before dinner with you family, or cuddling time with your loved ones. Your experiences will be greatly impacted by creating these energy flows.

## THIS IS HOW TO DO IT:

1. After conducting the breath technique for breath retention 'Kumbha', place your hands about a foot apart from each other. Allow yourself to feel the sensations of each hand passing through it. Slowly bring your hands together and notice the magnetic flow start to pull the energy to each other. After becoming familiar with these energies, slowly pull your hands about a foot apart again and you should start feeling the energetic connection between them. Do this a few times to keep the energy stream flowing. To break the energy flow when it's not wanted, I'd do this when interacting with people I don't know well or during work for the external world you can clap your hands together.

2. For a quick start after you get the energy flow going, you can rub your hands together vigorously, pull them apart to feel the energy flow…and then proceed with whatever you are using the energy in your hands for. I'd recommend this when cooking, for completing projects, tending to your children, etc.

# SPIRITUAL GIFTS AND THE ANAHATA

It is not surprising that the powers and energetic flow of the heart have been manipulated across mankind for centuries. This is what we were created for. The Anahata at its fullest capacity is an exceptional state of existence. But we have grown and been encouraged by slave owner mentality and indoctrination to be afraid of our capabilities because of our traumas. Because life works in cyclical circumstances, we can see this happening as we watch the occurrences play out at large within our world's stage. **We are each so traumatized, that we are fully functioning within oppression.**

Within this level of trauma and lack of access to education by those we have entrusted to carry out the good will of our species, we have been forced to not only function at low level energetic states within this generation, but we also carry episodic memories that last from generation to generation in a compounded fashion only making our traumas and the healing process with each generation harder. This is why we see disease rearing its ugly head the way we have and harder to battle. To end the cyclical cycles, we have to reach and maintain full operation of the heart space and the only way to do that is to heal our traumas.

When we heal, we heal at least fourteen generations back through our bloodline and can finally escape the death and rebirth cycle we have all been placed under recycling our energies back into these physical forms. **Some of us are here to do just that! To heal our generational bloodlines and free them of bondage.** Healing by touch is another gift of the Anahata as it relates to the heart by touch of hands. This process allows a clear individual to combine universal energies and Holy Spirit to allow themselves to be a conduit to channel energy to a direct source of physical or emotional ailment. **Reiki is an energetic resource that goes more in depth into the process of hands on healing**. As with any type of healing modality, there are varying layers of learning, real life application through the practice and growth of reiki. To each its own for the calling, but I personally believe Reiki to be one of the MOST effective ways to clear blocked and stored energy within our emotional bodies. My life, and the lives of many of my clients and students have changed once they implemented the art of Reiki as an additional hand on modality into their lives.

The other spiritual gift that is tied to the abilities of a free and clear heart is to be aroused to have an internal visual experience through touch of an individual's physical body or if it's strong enough, through another's auric field; this takes a clear and pure heart to do. This ability is called Clairtangency or Psychometry. These visions come as a flash through touch and connect you to the information you need related to the 'subject at hand.'

## SOCIAL PSYCHOLOGY

Positioning Theory- This subject looks at how an individual relates to or contributes to a group or community. It is a review of the social relatability of an individual and their environment. Using this theory within the Anahata discovery, will enable practitioners by the review of their client's environment and standing relationships to know exactly where and how their traumas are stored.

# ANAHATA HEALING MODALITIES

- Affirmations
- Breathwork
- Diet and Exercise
- Nature
- Qi Gong
- Reiki
- Running/Jogging
- Yoga

## PERSONAL TESTIMONY

The most pivotal time of my life was my diagnosis of my tumors and polyps. I wasn't going out like that and I luckily caught it early. I knew I had to implement radical changes and acknowledge all that had led me up to that point resulted with a broken heart. My circumstances did not create a blockage. They instead made my heart overactive. I never 'looked for love' per say, but I preoccupied myself with giving it in every way that I could. I only did this with people I felt I could trust in some way and it made me open game for narcissists of all kinds. As a child I did not have a close physical or emotional relationship with either of my parents. For their own reasons and their own struggles in life - with their own traumas - again, I do not blame them in any way. The reality is what it is. Not to mention, they were teenagers when they had me and didn't have a lot of life exposure beyond the experience of their own systemic traumas which again, where at no fault of their own. And we can clearly trace that back varying generations. As a result, like themselves and so many of us, they were unavailable in many ways.

*Their absence physically and/or emotionally and the acknowledgement that I had seen others have this level of support created blockages in many chakra regions and overactivity in others throughout my life. I would give freely from my heart, but never allowed anyone to get close enough to me to know the real me. I think the underlying emotional bondage this created for me was that I was unwanted. My relationship with my mother was always combative, and as a result, years later we've had to remove ourselves from those circumstances. Through that relationship and many others, I'd acquired as a result of being such a giving person but emotionally guarded I learned to set boundaries.*

*What I was blessed with as a result of my parent's inability to provide the level of care I needed. Especially a child like me, I was reading chapter books by the time I was three-years old and fully writing in cursive. I had a lot of questions and a vast memory at that tender age which only increased the older I got. I required a lot of guidance because of that. I think I was a lot for a young mother to handle and because she didn't know how and was dealing with her own healing and emotions, she unconsciously tuned me out. That is my belief anyhow. However, I was blessed to have my maternal Great Grandmother who embraced me and gave me all the nurturing I needed. She took the time to get to know me as a person and she also allowed me to get to know her. My great grandmother is the primitive basis of all that I am and my quest for knowledge.*

*My great grandmother Irene answered all of my questions and introduced me to everything I knew. She knew I was far more aware than most children my age and instead of forcing me to fit the mold, she encouraged me to step out of it. She was my spiritual guide, taught me unconditional love, and everything she herself had learned about life, love, and relationships as much as she could interpret for a small child. She was wise and did her best to give me everything I was lacking in guidance while still lovingly supporting my mother. My mother and I came up more as sisters. Don't get me wrong, she also made contributions to my life, but this is a fact that we cannot hide or deny. I wouldn't be who I've become without my great grandmother.*

*I was given my maternal grandmother, my nana and my uncle who was just fourteen years older than me. He was more like my big brother. My nana was more of a guide sent to help me understand the way of the world and how to navigate and identify personality traits in others that would eventually hurt me. Still to this day, she is all those things for me. Then, there was my paternal grandmother who taught me religion. She was the most loving person and God conscious individual in general that I have ever encountered. Still. She embraced and worked with the fact that I never fully claimed a specific religion but knew that I had a deep appreciation for the spiritual process and admire the true works and teachings of 'Jesus Christ.' She was the first person that encouraged me to face myself and sit with my traumas.*

*The day my life formally changed; I was 23-years old. I was feeling low and unwanted in the world after doing something I knew was extremely morally wrong but felt I had no other choice to do and I went to my paternal grandmother's apartment which was two streets over from mine. She looked at me and told me, saw and felt all of my pain. I couldn't hide it and I was emotionally crying for support. She cried and held me tight and looked deep into my spirit and said that I was filled with* anger. Defensively I stated that I was not. She said you are and gave me a sheet of paper and a pencil and told me to write. The number of things that poured through gave me an incredible release. That was my very first moment of surrender and where and when I accepted the responsibility of being fully accountable for my behaviors and the start of really becoming self-aware - something so many individuals are unfamiliar with as we are not being taught this process any longer - and again, narcissism is at an unsurpassed high.

*Fast forward to my diagnosis.* My diagnosis happened three-years from my maternal Great Grandmother's transition into the spirit realm. I held her hand while she transitioned. While this act was such an honor, being who she was to me, you can only imagine what that did to me emotionally. I trekked through life after that for a short while trying to cope and not letting anyone know I was hurting and that I felt more alone than ever before.

I changed my ways and became serious about my first son who was an infant at the time, my career, and my education doing everything I physically could to ensure that my son would have healthier life experiences. I stayed that way...surface level for a long time until I fell in love again, giving my all for the very first time in my life other than my children. But this circumstance brought up my emotional wounds and not a healthy loving relationship.

I forced myself to look at this aspect of myself and through a process of reflection and accountability, changed the behaviors I had taken on as a result of my upbringing. I was tested for all mental and personality disorders by two providers and was only diagnosed with PTSD. As a result, I knew what I was dealing with was internal and that I had to heal my broken heart in order to live again.

*I started to work on my emotions. I found a reiki practitioner after my diagnosis. My life and my children's lives desperately needed it. For the people who say that those who are raised on survival don't love well and to stay away from them, please stop saying that. Maybe you missed an assignment to help as long as they aren't toxic to your environment. This is what we are here for. To love unconditionally and it's okay for us to work through our trauma. But ultimately it is our own accountability.*

*After my first session the practitioner told me I had the natural gift of healing as well, but I already knew that from experience. That was another gift I tried to hide because people will attack anything they don't fully understand, and I still had not yet met anyone quite like me. I looked into reiki myself. Recovery from my heart space trauma took me years as there are so many layers to uncover. As a result of the various layers healing takes (this can be depicted in each of the lotus flowers in each chakra's symbol representation). It has taken work to manage and ensure I've set the appropriate boundaries to be able to work freely within this space and energy. I'm fully emerged in the space of unconditional love and ready to serve.*

*I've received the message through guidance that it is okay to serve wherever you are on your journey but in order to really help others you've got to operate with an open heart.* **Before you can really help anyone, you have to heal you without** *shame attached. **We all have room to heal.*** *Not every person's healing journey is as traumatic as mine, and some may even be deeper (I'll share my full story at another moment in time). It's the process of putting your own life vest on before you can help another person put theirs on. Why? Because otherwise you could drown. And so many of us are drowning with bottled up traumas we don't know how to release.*

*Today is a new day. It is your time to own our destiny again. To take back control over the fate of our lives and live lives full of abundance and love as we really are intended to be beyond the bondage.* ***Please be cautious not to ignore the assistance you are given and will in turn give others. No matter the hand it is coming from. Unconditional Love is everything and everything is love.***

I know interpersonal relationships can be hard and most definitely complicated. Let me gift the following meditation. It is my hope and desire that it helps you to foster GREAT interpersonal relationships.

Here is your meditation:
http://bit.ly/soiwokeup-harmonious-interpersonal-relationships

# SECTION III

TREE OF LIFE
BODY SYSTEMS
VISHUDDHA
THROAT CHAKRA TRAUMA
SOCIAL PSYCHOLOGY
THE MANDELA EFFECT/ FALSE MEMORY
AJNA
THIRD EYE TRAUMA
HEALING RESOURCES/ HATHA YOGA
EMOTIONAL ACCOUNTABILITY
DIMENSIONS
TREE OF LIFE/ METATRON'S CUBE
SAHASRARA
CROWN CHAKRA TRAUMA

# CHAPTER ELEVEN
# VISHUDDHA

## SO FAR, WE HAVE DISCUSSED:

- Muladhara/Root Chakra
- Svadhisthana/Sacral Chakra
- Manipura/Solar Plexus
- Anahata/Heart Chakra

## OF THESE ENERGETIC GATEWAYS WE HAVE COVERED:

- Correlating Functions/Body Systems
- Degrees of Consciousness
- Emotional Body
- Emotions
- Energy
- Healing Resources
- Sacred Geometry
- Social Psychology
- Soul Components
- Spiritual Guidance
- Tree of Life

I hope we are having fun! We have moved through the unconscious reality and its functions and have entered the domain of how these 'unconscious' patterns and cycles work through our emotional bodies contributing to the way we think about ourselves and relate to one another. We have discussed the varying aspects of the human soul, and the possibilities of operating in a pure level of consciousness. After attaining full consciousness and awareness of all possibilities that lie within the Anahata/heart energy, we now enter the domain of the Vishuddha/throat chakra. **Vishuddha is our own central purification center. Our source of truth.** This energy region is the manifestation of what our beliefs and emotions are. One's internal truth is found and exhibited through an individual here.

Ask yourself this question, "Is your reality real? What is your focus?" In relation to the tree of life, the Vishuddha is represented by the sephira's Gebura/Judgement and Severity and Chesed/Mercy and Love. Either of your internal truths will manifest themselves through these two aspects of the Vishuddha, and it is common that we each vacillate between these aspects of the Vishuddha's functions.

Chesed, sephira #4 represents Mercy and is a masculine energy. Chesed is also represented by Magnificence and is considered high in rank on the scale of universal energies. The God aspect of this sephira is "El" or El Elyon which means the most high God. Chesed, also displays the aspects of the human forgiving nature. **With this aspect of our soul's experience, this aspect in full function, is all we need in life to survive or win ANY battle.**

The Arch Angel associated to Chesed is Zadkiel, the angel of justice and the east winds. The realm of this sephira's function is the realm of brilliance. Chesed is the property of the emotional body that completes the second energetic trinity; completing the hexagram of energy flow we began discussing with the Anahata. This trinity combined represents the aspects of our consciousness that allow protection, forgiveness, and generosity. The functions of Chesed are tied to left arm/body functions. The planet is Pluto. Kabbalists define this quality as the 'Abys.'

Geburah is path #5 and represents strength and severity. The energy tied to this sephira is a magnetic feminine principle. The emanation of this sephira is projected in either one of two ways. Either it is an emanated quality combined with Chesed promoting communication of strength and severity that is tied with the properties of protection, forgiveness and generosity, or it is stand alone and provides an aspect of communication or truth that is strong and severe in nature and is reactive to lower level emotions of fear and with trauma ties, it will present as cruelty.

We get to decide how these aspects play out, and with a freely flowing emotional body, the ties of these qualities are exceptionally healthy. The aspect of God as represented in this sephira is Elohim Gebor, it means the all-powerful God and provides justice. In biblical reference, this is the aspect of God that supported David against Goliath through the coverage of ashes of penance. Elohim Gebor empowers each individual to be courageous and promote integrity. The Arch Angel that governs this sephira is Camael who is the angel that 'sees' God and governs power. The realm to which these qualities belong to is the realm/angelic order of the Seraphim which are fiery serpents (such as dragons) who guard the throne of God. The planet is Mars.

# BODY SYSTEMS

The Vishuddha functions govern the digestive system. This system, although not commonly communicated or recognized in this way, is a connection to the ears, nose, and throat. The digestive system takes in food and breaks down its nutrients allowing the nutrients to be absorbed through the blood. Yes, you really are what you eat…but most of us are learning that gravely as we search for many ways to combat disease.

Although additional attributes of the Vishuddha are represented through description of the senses, I'd like to associate them to the digestive process as their functions correlate to one another. Sound, hearing, or its formal title: Auditory Perception, is the process of our body receiving varying degrees of vibration. Sound/vibration can be heard and interpreted through solids, liquids, or gas. These signals and vibrations are perceived through a chemical process as these vibrations hold molecular compounds that exist within the depths of universal energies, down to cellular phones, to human and animal interaction; the cells within our bodies, and our energetic interactions with each other.

The sense of smell is in its totality a process of digestion that allows us as individuals to identify hazards (which associated to the Vishuddha creates fight or flight reactions), detection of pheromones although this is an unconscious process. This integrates with the sense of taste through use of the mouth and throat functions. Psychology describes the sense of smell as the 5th sense because the sense of smell as governed by the Vishuddha is associated to memory and emotion.

# THE VISHUDDHA

The Vishuddha/Throat chakra is the energy point of purification within our emotional body. It is associated with all qualities that identify as self-expression. A closed or blocked Vishuddha begins the process of death and decay or on the opposite end of the pendulum swing, can be the very productive transmutations of brilliance and learning. The chakra in particular, is closely identified with the successes and failures we experience in our lives. This energy port is the link to the beginning of the spine. Many associate this energy to the Akasha energy field and is the prominent reason for blockage of the kundalini experience for most as it correlates to each individuals personal and external truths.

The Vishuddha works in conjunction with an additional smaller chakra located at the roof of our mouths and is called Lalana. Its merits are identified in respect, contentment, offense, self-control, lack of pride and honor, disrespect, honor, sorrow, and joy. The Vishuddha is also associated with the thyroid glands and will have a faulty reaction to the thyroids in hyperactivity when one is not speaking their internal truths and hypoactivity when one is overly projecting their internal truths to their counterparts. The thyroid gland is also tied to the endocrine system and produces the hormones that are necessary for growth and maturation. In blockage or overactive qualities of this chakra, you will most certainly see these qualities.

# VISHUDDHA AND TRAUMA

When you see an individual, who is stuck at a particular age in life and not advancing, typically there is a blockage or overactivity here of some sort. A freely flowing throat chakra is represented by the elephant and all of its grace. The Vishuddha and the emotional body determine how well you communicate your emotions, the ability to handle conflict and confrontation, and your ability to live life authentically. Because most of our society has been blocked from full functioning upper chakras, the operation of low chakra functions has encouraged and almost blindly encouraged our species to pass down lifestyles that do not agree with our souls intended purpose and our destinies which has caused conflict and dysfunction at large. The blockage and programming is the reason that so many look at those of us that are dedicated to the work, the truth, or lightworkers working to service humanity as though we were crazy when in actuality, we are the ones who understand the truth, the intended human way, and the purification process of unified consciousness.

When we are functioning freely within the Vishuddha, we make ourselves understood in a great way. Blockage of this energy center can occur at any time and can last for short moments or as long as a physical body lifetime and sometimes even after the soul's transition into the energetic plane which can cause a soul to be stuck in the 4th dimension.

## TRAUMAS TO THE VISHUDDHA AND SIGNS OF BLOCKAGE ARE:

1. Dental Issues
2. Detachment/ Flight
3. Erratic hormone levels
4. Guilt
5. Habitual liars
6. Hearing Loss
7. Inconsistency with communication and the actions demonstrated.
8. Low self-esteem and lack of empowerment
9. Secrecy
10. Social Anxiety
11. Sore Throat and throat associated disease
12. Stiff neck
13. Stubbornness
14. Thyroid problems

## VISHUDDHA/THROAT CHAKRA

CHAPTER TWELVE

# SYNCHRONICITIES AND SOCIAL PSYCHOLOGY

**S**YNCHRONICITIES ARE A series of coincidences that can also be tied to social psychology. Psychologist Carl Jung has also famously recorded varying types of synchronicities but for the sake of the Vishuddha and understanding trauma recovery, we will review seven types. Jung identifies these happenstances as 'meaningful coincidences.' **Synchronicities are typically communications from our subconscious and higher selves that are keeping us on track with alignment. They can also be signs from angels and spirit guides. They are identifying a window of opportunity and will become sparse if they are neglected.** Operating in varying degrees of consciousness will also allow these occurrences to take place.

Quantum Physics associates this occurrence to the theory of the universal mind. The color of this realm is blue, and the HZ is 639 to 741 frequencies. Previously, we saw that the HZ associated to the chakra began to blend. The vibration of the Anahata to Vishuddha and increasing begins to become more defined. This frequency begins a world view perspective, that is beyond community-based consciousness and blends with ascended master energy.

1. **Number Repetition** - As we are seeing, the entire universe is made of numbers and patterns and is an additional form of communication beyond speech, and telepathy. Number synchronicities are typically the first type of synchronicity most awaken to. From my experience, it seems to be a precursor to a new level of awakening.

2. **Animals** - Because animals operate within a different realm of reality, they typically hold the frequency of cosmic resonance and instinctively understand how and when to communicate the wisdom of its totem. Because we also are associated with varying animals within the animal kingdom, the animals we see and associate with have great symbolism. Indigenous tribes often correlate this meaning and symmetry and have not lost the art of the wisdom communicated through animals as a totem.

3. **Deja-Vu** - Déjà vu is having an experience in life for a second time. It is a clear indication that time is fluid and not linear. Everyone experiences déjà vu. It is knowing what is about to happen and having a perfect recall of the conversation, people, places, or things that are associated to it.

4. **Knowing** - This synchronicity is tied to the ability to know or call a person, place, or thing and then it actually happens. For example, you can say...the phone is ringing...and the phone rings. Or to say someone's name or speak of them and then they call. This is synchronicity.

5. **Music or verbal communication** - I believe this synchronicity has mostly to do with spirit. You may be thinking of something and a song that either correlates to your current emotion or answers your feeling comes on. This is the reason I always have music playing. Sometimes, I am channeling, even while having everyday conversation and need/prefer the music playing so that I know I'm on track.

6. **Answer Interception** - This occurrence is when a message is received as an answer or insight through a third person about a personal question or given a verbal answer to question or a prayer. It is when a particular person seems to be brought into your life for a specific reason.

7. **Dreams** - There is a realm of dreams in itself. But within this realm, you can be given glimpses of an occurrence through your dreams. These dreams will consist of a similar or same recurring theme over again and typically relate to a phase in life you are in or moving into. Typically, the dream is metaphoric. This is another common occurrence of synchronicity for a newer awakening soul.

## SPIRITUAL GIFTS

The spiritual gifts associated with the throat chakra are Clairgustance, and Clairalience. **Clairgustance is when an individual receives information through their sense of taste.** Typically, this gift will associate a person and a topic through eating a specific food or drinking a drink. This gift will also produce keen sense of a peculiar taste when a need of guidance occurs, and they will, in turn, identify they are or are not on the appropriate path. Some have reported the taste of blood, chemicals, or sand and grit in their mouths. Clairalience is when an individual can smell a certain fragrance that exists at a higher dimension not identified by the average peer. Typically, these occurrences happen when an individual perceives a presence from another realm.

**The gift of tongues.** A fully functioning Vishuddha allows the ability for one to speak in tongues or as some describe it as light langue. Tongues or light langue is not only the ability to communicate effectively in a pattern of speech that others cannot understand but can be understood by spirit; it is also the ability to understand different dialects of langue through hearing. In legends, folktales, it is said that the communication and gathering of people to again begin the process of 'Christ consciousness' on the day of Pentecost was the day that the langue of man was broken up into differing dialects.

CHAPTER THIRTEEN

# PYRAMIDS

**IT IS BELIEVED** that pyramids and temples were constructed as a means to communicate to the 'gods.' As depicted in the biblical story of the tower of Babylon. I have to be transparent here, I do not believe this story. I believe that it was created or included within the context of the bible to incite and provoke fear for the knowledge of the order and kingdom of heaven and higher dimensional existence. For example, the United States stands by the note that the country was built on the ethics of Christianity, but the demonstration of pyramids and towers are found all over the world and is largely depicted throughout western culture. Is there a truth to the power that pyramids, and temples hold that the 'elite' do not want the rest of humanity to know?

One of the most popular pyramids we have come to be familiar with within western society is that which is depicted on the dollar bill. It is most popularly known to be the 'eye of province.' It is also seen as the work of the Freemasons. The terms that float above the floating eye above the pyramid structure are 'Annuit Coeptis' which are Latin and mean, "*He* has favored our undertakings." At the base of this temple are the roman numerals for the year that the seal was passed as the United States financial emblem. And beneath the pyramid in a scroll, are the Latin words, "Novus Ordo Seclorum" which translates to mean, "The new order of the ages."

Ever ask yourself why is this image on the American dollar? Could this be related to a pyramid scheme ideology? Or even The Global Wealth Pyramids? Something to think about.

Many believe the pyramids that are seen in repetition throughout our history have been historical store houses for grains and varying dry goods for their communities and also to be burial grounds for gods and kings. As time continues scientists and archeologists are finding more and more pyramids throughout the world, with the latest discovery that I've been made aware of as the discovery of pyramids in Turkey. Some of these pyramids are actually inverted beneath the earth. There are pyramids all over the earth. There are also pyramids on the Moon and on Mars...It is being discovered, as also taught by Thoth, that pyramids and temples have the same energetic functionality that we have the ability to achieve within our own energy bodies with Merkabah. These sacred sites have been a portal to connect to other realms of reality and dimensions. This is the same function as our Ajna/third eye.

The location of these pyramids, temples, and other sacred sites align and intersect with the highest points of energy integration and in relation to the consciousness grid that surrounds the earth further extending into other dimensions. The pyramids and temples also exist on access ports and vortexes inside the earth in locations that correlate to the same chakra energy system that runs throughout each of us. The structure of these energy ports also further correlates to the same tree of life structure that surrounds us and governs each of us. The question posed now is…why hasn't this information been shared at large? Why has it been hidden? To answer this, I will state that it is time to awaken from the deep sleep we have been subjected to. The Ajna, performs as our own internal pyramid or temple, linking our conscious mind with the subconscious and our higher selves, or also known as the over soul. We recognize once we awaken that the $4^{th}$ dimension is a dream state. The $3^{rd}$ dimension is a state of deeper sleep. Again…it's time for us to wake up.

The sciences as we know them today, have been available and have been accessible through these pyramids as energy vortexes. The true function of pyramids that do in fact correlate to the human soul's functions. Pyramids are built with limestone, mineral stones, and crystals. **Limestone is a source of electrical energy**. These electrical generation of free energy sources is what Tesla mastered and attempted to teach humanity. We have replicated these functions with our towers that we see in varying places all over the place especially within western cultures. These materials and positioning on these vortex energy portals, is what generates the energy needed for them to function as energy sources. The question left here is, has the functionality of these pyramids and temples been dismantled or are they still intact and waiting to be activated?

Oddly enough, global governments have taken hold of artifacts founds within these sacred sites and have held most of the knowledge found within them secret. The roman catholic church, and other religious organizations, have invaded civilizations that have historically functioned within the temple and pyramid atmosphere and ravished and destroyed historical artifacts that hold key pieces of information of our ancient history. Why is that? Even if we don't care, the synergy between the functionality and the human body are undeniable. Because of the intensity involved within the functions of the pyramids, could they also be used to sypher energy out of species? Although it is mostly discussed with the pyramid of Giza, the pyramids have a sacred geometry equation that equal to the 'Golden Number.'

# RATIO/ENERGY OF THE GOLDEN NUMBER

# WHAT IS THE GOLDEN NUMBER?

1. Phi which is the ratio that repeats itself throughout nature.
2. Pi which is the circumference of a circle in relation to the diameter.
3. The Pythagorean Theorem.

These ratios are important to know, because they include the ratio of Pi which has a value that is impossible to know…Much like what we have come to know about the power and grace of Elohim and our universe, correct? But these elements are here within our lives. Pi ratios always stay the same. It is the most important number in the universe.

# THE MANDELA EFFECT

We as a species, have all been enslaved. All of us, even the ones we see as oppressors of varying kinds. The breakdown of the Ajna is how we have all been enslaved into a systemic cycle of abuse and trauma keeping us linked to root level 3rd dimensional consciousness even with all of our access to information and with the use of modern-day technology. **The Mandela Effect or false memory is the biggest form of abuse and trauma our species has faced. False memory is when an individual believes and remembers an event or fact or has a recurring emotion as a result of something that did not actually exist or happened very differently from the way it actually happened.**

This is the impact that causes our species to live in a dualistic state. Our species has been battling itself on an internal level causing us to become stuck and enslaved participants to the system and structure we have been placed under reinforcing the trauma we endure as a species; to keep us operating from a space of oppression. It is overstated I am aware, but it is necessary in order for us to understand what has happened to the human species. Because our memory recall and our connection to spirit in true essence has been tampered with, we have been easily controlled and manipulated keeping us from a true state of unified consciousness within our planet and suppressing our nature as Christ Conscious individuals which we all have a right to. Instead, we have become enslaved to the world's financial system.

The Mandela Effect is typically represented by the distortion of two major categories. **First being that of 'verbatim.'**

**This is the actual recall with a justified reasoning for a lasting impact to an emotional state; for an individual account of an occurrence or experience.** Then there is the gist representation which causes an inflated or blanket effect as a result of an occurrence or experience. Typically, false memories as a result of the Mandela Effect are in fact related to low level energies and emotional states, threshold trauma, and trauma bonds.

Duality can be described as we have previously referenced, as an altered state of existence as a result of the Mandela Effect. Shadow aspects of life in driving our lives forward through the manipulation of unconscious thought patterns by overtaking our true nature as souls within a subconscious state. Remember, "As above, so below."

Everything that takes place in higher dimensional spaces happens in replica within our lives in this third dimensional reality. Gaslighting has become extraordinarily popular and has become very common as the energies pervade the human species and attach themselves to dark entities and overtangle structures through fraudulent governmental structures, dogmatized religious structures, access to dramatized reality TV programs, addiction to technology, and a competitive nature for individuals to keep up with the Kardashians (I objectively believe this family is living out their purpose), or faking it until they make it instead of living in their own purpose have these individuals falling victim to the matrix grid system. Gaslighting is an extension of the Mandela Effect, and while it is largely an attribute of the class B personality disorders, it is becoming the way of our civilization and needs large eradication. For this, we have to heal our traumas.

**Basically, gaslighting is a form of psychological manipulation associated as an extension of the Mandela Effect that discredits the integrity of a culture, community, event, historical nature, or even an individual.** All of these outlined implications of gaslighting are common and relevant in each and every one of our everyday lives. Our species has been subjected to much of this. The impacts of this Mandela Effect system have caused so much threshold trauma within the spirit of each of us, that is breaking us down and shaking us into states of awareness at vast rates. I find this statement in association to gaslighting as a perfect fit as it relates to the overarching energies from a matrix grid system, to overtangle structures, to individuals with compound trauma structures to be very relevant. The definition of gaslighting via Wikipedia is as follows, "Using persistent denial, misdirection, contradiction, and lying, gaslighting involves attempts to destabilize the victims and delegitimize the victim's beliefs." As found in Wikipedia.

When we are operating in a conscious/subconscious state of mind, it is not likely that we may fall victim to the circumstances that the Mandela Effect attempts to pervade into our lives. The Mandela Effect is also a form of pyramid scheme system. It is the current structure our society operates from at large and has caused the destruction of so many communities, cultures, and even families. As I personally continued to awaken from the matrix system and continued to reach extended levels of subconscious, I have watched these energies pervade and persist forcing many to operate in ways that are against their true nature. Not even realizing that they have fallen victim to an over tangle structure of darkness that seeks to keep individuals stuck in a state of trauma.

Recalling back to our initial context, there is nothing anyone can do to help awaken the individuals who are operating under these structures. We each have to seek and be responsible for our own salvation and actually know what that really means. Not the way we have been taught and has been largely accepted. We can, however, send loving energy to those who have fallen victim of the Mandela Effect in these varying ways and proceed with caution. All we can do is be a model to the wonderful world of awareness and consciousness and be great examples of love and light and $5^{th}$ dimensional consciousness. Afterall, that's where we are headed anyway.

## SOCIAL PSYCHOLOGY

The Mandela Effect is the trauma we are discussing at large as it is the trauma that every single one of us has experienced. **The Skeleton Theory as it relates to the social psychology of false memory or gaslighting is based on the memory recall process and is broken down to acquisition and retrieval.** The acquisition is an individual's process of taking in a small piece of any given experience while ignoring the totality of the experience. It's somewhat of a state affixation. This process links the event to this specific targeted affixation or focal point rather than the full experience creating a blockage. The retrieval process of this information dictates the reaction to the individual's environment making the experience internal as a result of the blockage and project the internal processing or the actual event. The outcome in emotional processing and relationship discretion is then determined by either the facts associated to the events as they have occurred or the false memory. Comprehension and communication through open energy channels related to the Vishuddha and the Ajna create an appropriate path of communication and perception at this point.

## THE AJNA

The Ajna is the entry port of the subconscious level of existence. Because of the realities we face today the functions of this energy system, have been split into one of a dualistic nature as well. So many of us have come to learn that this gland has been calcified by the use of fluoride and other programming we have been subjected to as a species. I believe that television programs, foods, inappropriate iodine intake (salts, etc.), artificial light resources, energy manipulation, the Mandela Effect (matrixed programming), and trauma, have all contributed to the calcification of the Pineal gland which is also tied to the Ajna energy port. The Ajna/third eye is an internal eye that is our link to perception beyond visible sight. Ajna means to perceive and to command in Sanskrit. The color of the third eye is indigo, the sound frequency is HZ 852- 963.

It is the mind's eye and can be accessed through deep meditation and practice of varying spiritual systems that focus on individual consciousness largely within the practices of Buddhism and Taoism through the practice of stoicism. I personally have practiced stoicism within the beginning stages of my own personal awakening, and I am eternally grateful as I gained a vast amount of self-awareness and was able to then begin to change my behaviors and remove myself from low levels of consciousness and unconscious emotional ties and relationships. Hindu recognizes this sacred energy port through the use of a Bindi. A bindi is a sacred process of decorating an individual's

Ajna energy area externally with a red dot. To the Hindus, it is the access point that represents creation and its celebration through the bindi represents unity. To do this, Hindus use their ring finger on their left hand to symbolize the connection of the heart to the third eye in representation of unified consciousness. I revere this process as it is beautiful.

The Ajna/pineal gland is made up of small calcite crystals (yes... yes... yes... you are also a crystalline being) that contain calcium, carbon, and oxygen. Because it is a crystalline structure, it also maintains a consciousness in of itself, combining with the soul level of consciousness. The other crystal we have within our bodies is the Otoconia crystals, which are in our ear canals and also link to the Ajna functions through the Vishuddha/throat chakra and further link to our spinal cord. Otoconia crystals respond to the earth's gravitational pull and give us balance. An individual with a high otoconia receptivity and energy flow are those individuals that can channel information beyond this level of perception because of the potency of their frequency and clear energy flows.

The calcite crystals within the pineal gland, interact with the electromagnetic fields surrounding us and in advanced individuals, universally, allowing one access to perceive time and space through the wavelength frequencies. Pretty cool right? Just as your perceptual eye does, the pineal gland also has a lens, cornea, and retina. The pineal gland is also the source of your melatonin. The calcites within the pineal gland, when decalcified, produce and internal light that regulates your body's sleep cycle, stress level, and connects further to the endocrine system. Because melatonin produces darkness, it is helpful to further decalcify your pineal gland while meditating in the dark. It is through the Ajna, that the electromagnetic energy within each of us produces energy once we have clear energy flows and provides functionality to this amazing wonder within the human body. I hypothesize given the functions of the Ajna, the appropriate body system that correlates is the circulatory system.

The pituitary gland known as the 'seat of the mind' is also maintained within the functions of the Ajna energetic port. In combination to the third eye, this gland functions and can be activated just as the pineal gland to help aid and regulate hormones and furthermore, emotional responses. Because of the high electromagnetic interaction within the Ajna system, this gland regulates hormone productivity of the growth hormone, testicles, ovaries, menstrual periods, sexual feelings, thyroids, and fertility. Individuals experiencing difficulties in these areas could also use clearing work on the third eye to open or bring balance to any or all these areas. The fall out of these energy maintenances results in pituitary disorders.

The pituitary gland is the psychic source within us. The pineal gland is the perception of the connection to the pituitary gland. I am sure to include the pituitary gland in each of my sessions with my healing clients as this is not subject matter than is widely taught. The imbalance of the Ajna, pineal gland and pituitary gland create severe brain trauma which result in disorders as mild as lack of discernment to as extreme as Alzheimer's condition. Science and medicine do not know the cause of these conditions and have no solution other than medication to suppress the process. I hypothesize that with the appropriate treatment methods and clearings of the Ajna, these diseases can be wildly eradicated. As a primary descendant of the genetic condition I have taken a sincere personal interest on these disorders and have implemented techniques on myself and my clients that help with these stimulants to help reduce the exposure to these diseases, but I know for a fact, healing trauma is the first step to eradicating the process.

## AJNA/ THIRD EYE CHAKRA

CHAPTER FOURTEEN

# TREE OF LIFE

**THE HERMETIC PRINCIPLE** that ties to the Ajna is 'The All in All.' It states, "To him who truly understands this truth hath come great knowledge." The energy that exists with this statement and level of consciousness is the understanding of which means so much. This truth is the multitude of all truths of philosophical, scientific, and religious origin. The aspects of the tree of life that govern the Ajna are sephira #3 Binah/Understanding and #2 Chokmah/Wisdom. These exciting aspects depict the appropriate functioning of duality that have been altered and tampered with in modern existence.

Sephira #3 Binah/Understanding holds a feminine energy in which is a passive and mailable quality. It is also called Ama which means mother in the Hebrew langue. Marah representing the tides and waves of the sea, and Mary representing the Mother of All. This sephira is the bliss of the feminine properties of Elohim. Within the sephiras Binah and Chokmah the essence of sex and chemistry is created and as a result they represent space and time. The God name associated with this aspect of the soul and universal energy flows is Jehovah Elohim which means Lord God. The representation of Jehovah Elohim is an infinite expression of Jehovah and is God representing His own intimate force. In biblical representation, Jehovah Elohim is depicted as carrying Noah through the flood. The Arch Angel governing Binah is Arch Angel Zaphkiel has many many translated names but the most common is Zaphiel. The order and realm of the sephira is the order of the thrones which is characterized by the qualities of peace and submission and exists in the universal realm where material forms begin to take place.

Sephira #2 is Chokman/Wisdom. Chokman has a masculine active energy and initiates the true essence of unity. It is also referenced as the Super Natural Father, and it is in itself the Zodiac. The God aspect of this sephira is Jehovah; it is also referred to in Hebrew traditions as Tetragrammaton; which has no translation, correlation, or definition because it is believed that the name of God is incomprehensible. Jehovah is the manifestation of all of creation in elemental reign as the universe, zodiac, fire, water, air, and earth all of which constitutes the energy of life.

Chokman is the force of wisdom that connects perfection of knowledge and understanding. The Arch Angel governing these energies is Ratziel who is the keeper of the secrets and miracles of the angels, lords, and gods. The realm governed within this sephira is the realm of the wheels, or I would translate as vehicle. This is the realm that sits just under the realm of the throne as governed by Binah.

The paths that connect Binah/Understanding and Chokman/Wisdom can also be identified and related to by the process of fetal development. If you've never watched a video that demonstrates the process, please watch as you are reviewing these paths. The synergy is remarkable. The paths are 11, 12, 13, 14, 15, 16, 17, and 18:

- **Path 11** - Path 11 is 'Scintillating Intelligence' and connects Chokman and Kether. This path signifies the veil that separates man and material beings of angelic order.
- **Path 12** - 'Intelligence of Transparency' connects Binah and Kether. This is the path of the wave of existence and time and allows the element of prophecy.
- **Path 13** - 'Uniting Intelligence' connects Kether and Tiphareth while intersecting Chokman and Binah. This path is the Glory. This unity defines the truth of spirituality. It is orgasmic. Creation. This path also begins the process of soul related relationships.
- **Path 14** - 'Illuminating Intelligence' connects Binah and Chokman. These are the stages of preparation of holiness or wholeness.
- **Path 15** - 'Constituting Intelligence' connects Chokman and Tiphareth and is the substance of creation in pure darkness.
- **Path 16** - 'Triumphal or Internal Intelligence' connects Chokman to Chesed which is the incomparable Glory. It is paradise.
- **Path 17** - 'Disposing Intelligence' connects Binah to Tiphareth and is the beginning of the embodiment of the holy spirit. Embodying the essence of pure faith beyond realization.
- **Path 18** - 'House of Influence' connects Binah and Geburah which is the path of abundance and where all senses and spiritual gifts are emanated through realization.

# THE BODY SYSTEMS AND THE AJNA AND HOW YOGA CAN HELP

An overactive or blocked Ajna will absolutely occur if any of the chakra energy systems below it are blocked or overactive. Because the Ajna connects the circulatory system, we will see cases of high cholesterol, diabetes, or high or low blood pressure. These are the most common ailments western societies face. These diseases are also largely undetected and undiagnosed. Yoga compresses and decompresses the veins and circulatory system within our body which allows for even energy distribution which flushes the blood and reveres the blood flow. Whether you have one of the conditions listed above or a fall out symptom that eludes to an Ajna blockage like exhaustion, severe cramping, swelling, brittle hair and nails, eye pain, blurred vision, or dark circles under the eyes, yoga will help reduce the risk of these dysfunctions and furthermore, help to break down stored trauma in the emotional body. Further freeing us to get connected onto path 18 as much as possible.

# PSYCHIC ATTACK

What exactly is a psychic attack? A psychic attack is when an individual intentionally or unintentionally sends dark and negative energy to another individual. Just as Pranic energy or reiki use the basis of love energy through universal flow to promote healing and balance, this can be done on the dark side to promote negativity and chaos in an individual's life. Typically, these individuals are highly clairsentient (commonly described as empaths) and because they have the ability to feel so strongly, they have the ability to 'throw' or project negative energy onto an individual or community of individuals. Psychic attacks can be encouraged by a dark entity, a spirit, overtangle of thought forms (egregors which we will discuss in detail in later context), but are typically an energetic attack by an extraordinarily strong mind that touches our auric fields in some way or can alter any and everything around it. The individuals who conduct these acts are typically referred to as energy vampires.

Because auras are weakened by repressed emotions, unresolved traumas, and ego-based activity, these attacks create dilating reactions to the implications in a cause and effect fashion. It is the type of scenario when nothing in your life seems to be working…Repetitious events of misfortune, memory loss, lack of energy, nightmares, feeling your being watched, things being broken, loss after loss, failure after failure can often be related to a psychic attack. Psychic attacks are typically created through an energy of obsession combined with extreme anger or extreme jealousy. It is rare that an individual has to perform actual magic to carry out these intentions but will absolutely be mentally and ethereally strong. Being the victim of a psychic attack by someone who is fixated on an individual and is also mentally strong is very scary. Psychic attacks can also be self-inflicted by repetitive thought patterns of severe negativity, anxiety, and fear-based belief systems.

Psychic attacks cause a ripple or wrinkle in time and tear through a vibrational currency and project negative energy at any given person place or thing. Sudden glass or objects breaking, explosion of light bulbs, randomly falling objects, sounding alarms, sudden clumsiness, or unexplained injuries are the most common side effects of this. Psychic attacks are the most common negative emotion that exists. For example, China, Russia, and now the USA have all trained their militaries on psychic attack strategies. Soldiers are currently being trained on how to read and control minds telepathically and then to manipulate minds, so the subject or person does what they want them to do. This is also a form of psychic attack. Russia has been conducting these activities the longest...This right here is not only a violation of many sorts but is worthy of a whoa faced emoji reaction.

**Psychic attacks** are often combined with roots magic and can really wreak havoc on an individual's life as combining the dark and negative energy to a dark and controlling entity. Exposure to a psychic attack is extremely strong after sex especially casual sex with an uncommitted partner. To combat a psychic attack, one must properly acknowledge their own emotions and do the work necessary to create and maintain clear energy flows, and deal with stress, disappointment, or anger appropriately. With a strong and healthy aura these types of attacks cannot impact an individual and you will know immediately once and if you are clear that this is in fact being done to you. **Psychic attacks can however alter the mental state of anything around an individual if an individual or a place does not have a strong aura or strong energetic shield of protection. This fact alone brings a whole new level of awareness to being careful who you surround yourself with or the company you keep.** Simply put...do the work. And surround yourself with others who are also doing their work. This eliminates or minimizes the likelihood of a psychic attack impacting your life in any way shape or form.

Spiritual Gifts associated to the Ajna are the most popular spiritual gifts and the most commonly acknowledged. Clairvoyance, prophecy, dreams, imaginations, visions... etc. This gift allows us to process mental images to align with the wave of time through the Ajna/third eye. Some see the colors of energy fields. Please be aware, without the work of healing, true release, and having a clear emotional body, this gift will be an internal projection of you...not unified consciousness and that's okay for some people but if we are to awaken to the levels of consciousness we are meant to achieve, your prophecies may help a few, but they will only be intended truly for and through your own perspective. This gift also allows an individual to visualize the solution to a problem. Clairvoyance can be a gift that combines all of the aforementioned spiritual gifts. Some clairvoyants can see the past, present, future, or even remote view. The topic of clairvoyance can be a book all in itself. It is my strongest gift.

## PERSONAL TESTIMONY

*This was my earliest remembered clairvoyant experience. It was the first time I recall that I used my ability to see through all time and space. When I was five-years old, I lived in Washington DC. My mother had taken me to Boston for a visit and introduced me to her then boyfriend. He gave me the creeps as soon as I saw him. There was something about his energy that I couldn't trust. I recall being in the backseat of his car. At some point during our visit, he got out of the car and left my mother and me alone. Once he was out of sight I jumped up and leaned forward and said, "Mommy please don't trust him he's bad." She looked at me perplexed and asked me to clarify what I was talking about.*

I told her that I didn't know but that I could feel it and that I could see that he does something that's bad. She again asked me to clarify what I was referencing. I told her I could see him smoking something bad that was not cigarettes and that it was in a shoe box at the bottom of the closet. I told her he was a bad man and that he would ruin our lives...she told me to shush and not say those things and he was soon back at the car. I sat back and shut my mouth and pouted the rest of the time... This began to happen a lot. When my mother tried to silence something, I could see or felt and I would often get an attitude until I learned to keep my visions to myself. I learned quickly that the world outside of my great grandmother, was not usually ready to receive what I saw.

Fast forward, my mother ended up marrying this man and he absolutely did everything that I saw. He destroyed our lives. He had a crack cocaine addiction that would destroy our lives and introduce us as children to the depths and darkness of a life we are not intended to experience.

By the time I was eleven-years old, I was living back in Boston with my mother, and after a typical drug binge of his, my mother decided she had enough and began to pack up his belongings. I sat silently in a chair in her room while she packed up his clothing from the closet. As she packed, she got to the bottom of the closet, the last shoe box that was there and she opened it...There was a crack pipe. She looked at me deeply; spoke no words, put the lid back on the shoe box, packed it away and never said another word of it. But I knew she knew...Although she didn't give feedback often, she began to listen a little more, but she never became a full supporter, which made me take a long *time to fully allow anyone to see me in that way again...Until I could not hide it anymore. But again... don't get me wrong, she just didn't know at the time what she didn't know, because she too like us all, had come from a place of trauma.*

*My mother's ex-husband fought many demons. He was verbally abusive because he was a liar and a master manipulator, physically abusive, although he never hit us, he was built like a bodybuilder and used his stature as intimidation attempting to ensure that we did not ever underestimate the power of his strength by destroying our home and stealing our personal belongings. And worst of all, he was sexually abusive, not only molesting me, but his own blood children as well and today I suspect (although never confirmed) he molested and carried out sexual relationships with my peers as well. I instead began to use this gift to create from what I saw within my visions and applied it to the many experiences I've had in life...*

CHAPTER FIFTEEN

# EMOTIONAL ACCOUNTABILITY

**T**HE TOPICS WE are discussing are not new age or theories. The information within these pages are evidence-based facts and these facts, in this understanding of order, are just the beginning to opening of new levels of consciousness. Once we evolve to a space where we have fully garnered self-awareness of the Sahasrara/crown chakra, moving us beyond a space of unconscious thought processes of the program, we evolve within our first trinity, to full consciousness and build healthy relationships not just with ourselves, but to the communities in which we live and belong to.

# SAHASRARA/CROWN CHAKRA

The next phase in our evolution becomes awareness of all that is. We start to become the galactic beings we are actually meant to be.

At this stage we are ready to accept all accountability of our roles in events, positive and negative, that we have experienced in life, come to a level of understanding and begin the process of working through our traumas and transmuting the energy that surrounds us into a positive energy that spreads the energy of unconditional love. We drop the need to force our will and our own agendas and begin to move with the natural ebb and flow of life. All experiences in our lives are driven to provide us with the highest level of learning possible, thus, enhancing our state of consciousness. If we've attained a healthy unity consciousness through a fully functioning Anahata and healthy external perception of the Ajna/third eye functionality we will successfully proceed to begin/to become enlightened to all there is beyond our comprehension. We will stop creating devices of division and unify all that we encounter. As we know and are gradually becoming to accept emotionally as we take the steps necessary to heal our wounds, we are eternal beings in which energy transforms. Our souls do not die.

This level of emotional maturity allows us to be internally joyful and that state of maturity will undoubtedly have an impact on our environment. Emotional accountability demonstrates the utmost level of respect and trust, first for your life and secondly to the world. This is real peace. This is the final state of being free of trauma. Not that you won't have experiences that are trying to your emotional wellness, but more than that, you will understand how to process what you've experienced to move forward in a healthy way. The time is now. Proper resolution and understanding of our past wounds allow us to fully unite with the aspect of our higher selves and for many of us, it allows us to fully connect to our souls.

# DIMENSIONS

Depending on where you research you will find information showing anywhere from 5-12 dimensions of consciousness although there are in fact even more than twelve. We will discuss twelve dimensions including the dimension we are currently in.

What is a dimension of reality? A dimension is a level of consciousness made up of vibration and frequency. Of these vibrations and frequencies there are about 144,000 as noted by many quantum physicists. Each dimension is a realm of reality that matches the same vibrational possibilities within the soul's emotional body and beyond. Within these dimensions are beings with varying degrees of universal energetic consciousness including extra-terrestrials, angels, lords, gods, and Source.

Frequency is everything in existence and it is defined as, "The rate at which a vibration occurs that constitutes a wave, either in a material (as in sound waves), or in an electromagnetic field (as in radio waves and light), usually measured per second." As defined in Wikipedia. Essentially, everything in existence is sound which resonates vibration. This is why the functions of the Svadhisthana (sacral chakra) and the Vishuddha (throat chakra) are the essence of truth through our creation. Our ability to create using these functions is why many classify our species as being made in God's image. Although I, like many, prefer to classify man as co-creators.

The purpose of living that we each share is actually to evolve as much in consciousness allowing us each to reach one's soul potential within this physical reality as a united body. Not as individuals where we see the strife and struggle of the world at large today is impacting us. From this level of unity, we are then meant to transcend to our highest form of consciousness within these physical vessels to then transcend returning into our pure energetic form of vibration. Our souls come into this dimension by choice for the most part. Not only is this a choice but your soul and level of consciousness, connect to each of these realms throughout any given phase and experience within our lives.

The 1st dimensional time and space can be considered by the use of an analogy of a neutron, or a seed, or even sperm. It is the start of the creation of a material form. Within our lives in physical form, this dimension is that of the soul star chakra energy.

2nd dimension is the realm of information. This is the realm in which we start to see code form. Where the numeric and sacred geometry of chance and values of creation begin to combine to later hold a denser material form. Second dimension holds a charge similar to that of a neuron but gives each of the species holding consciousness its genetic code and ethereal imprint. This dimension can also be analogized by the function of an unfertilized egg. Second dimension is beneath the earth itself and can be correlated to root chakra energy. The orgasmic static of this stage of awareness is what I often call and teach as a state of drama.

3rd dimension is the realm of manifestation of material and physical form. Here, our analogy can be the electron's combination with a proton and a neutron in its creation of an "Atom." This is the parable behind the biblical story of Adam and the garden. It's the same thing. Here our energy loses malleable energetic form and we enter our denser physical reality. Because the reality of the 3rd dimension is a dense matrix reality, it is hard for this level of consciousness to perceive any consciousness beyond this world. Most of the human species has been perceiving life at this level of consciousness and this dimension relates to the sacral chakra and can correlate to trauma.

4th dimension is the realm that best correlates to dreams. This is the dimension that holds our subconscious mind. It is also the realm that holds the most manipulative activity of the program we have been succumbed to. This is the realm just beyond our reality and begins the state of spirit. Astral projection becomes possible at this stage and can continue within each dimension from this stage. This is also where transcended souls become stuck to recycle into the grid if they have not succeeded 3rd dimensional consciousness. As, Pope Francis and Pope John Paul II declared in his dying days, there is no such as hell, but if there were, this and the 3rd dimension would be the closest things to it.

5th dimension is where we are currently headed as a society. This is where and how we connect to our higher selves and merge with great spirit. We are in full alignment when we reach a state of 5th dimensional level of consciousness. This is the start of what can be defined as 'heaven' or 'paradise.'

6th dimension is believed to be that of light. Within each level of consciousness that precedes the 6th there is a stage of surrender required to get to the next stage after the emotional body is clear of blockage. This is the realm that ascended masters reside. This dimension can also determine the path of a soul. Whether or not you begin again or move forward within consciousness. Some believe this process is a choice.

7th dimension is the realm where angels and angelic beings dwell. Angels move through realms and dimensions easily. This realm is the reality that occurs when the soul is ready to evolve. This dimension of consciousness will link you directly to your soul's individual divinity from the very start.

8th dimension is the universe. It is the realm of the lords. There are many lords that we have been denied access to; they are full of information among the varying cultures we have within the human species. Celebration is due here. Every dimension we experience up this point merge to create a new level of unity.

9th dimension is the realm of deity consciousness.

10th dimension is the realm of the Multiverse and the start of Melchizedek level of consciousness.

11th dimension is beyond comprehension. It is the realm that gives the soul the next level of existence.

12th dimension is the realm of Elohim. This is the ultimate level of love consciousness. This is the ultimate level of consciousness and is transmutation at its purest form. This level of consciousness permeates all over levels of consciousness. It is unity with all that is.

# SOULS

Contrary to popular belief, we are operating in free will when we are in alignment with our souls' purpose. The reason we chose to come here. That is actually what free will is. And most of the soul conscious beings here, came here now to help ascend the planet to at least a 5th dimensional consciousness as a whole. Because the atmosphere within the third dimension is such a dense reality, we have been robbed of our souls' memories and plugged into the 'grid.' We then interpret this reality's free will of being that in which we make it. This belief is what causes the soul to regenerate into this system over and over again.

Not everyone here is a being with soul deep consciousness. Some of the beings here and others within the animal kingdom, do not have souls. They are a mirrored result of an energetic creation. And there are some of us who do have souls. Scientists have calculated that roughly 85% of our population have souls. There are also some people here that have an incredible amount of demonic possession from entities that exist in 2nd dimensional and 4th dimensional consciousness, but the program has us labeling these individuals (usually with a class b personality type) further keeping us tied to this grid. With no judgement, some of our neighboring beings have originated energies from other sources. I don't wish to elaborate further on these energies. But I will share this bit of information.

As a result of my personal calling as an energetic healer and prophet, I've seen these types of attacks on so many within my own healing journey; turning even family and close loved ones and friends into enemies and within the lives of my clients. Darkness is real and there are so many souls and soulless portals that are being used as a tool of manipulation and they have been labeled and it's time to do something about it. Are you awake yet?

**Healing our traumas from our personal life experiences, our communities, and healing from the program we have been victim to is the way.** If this is something you'd like to look further into, you can. My stance on this topic is the following, in order to attain the highest level of consciousness possible, it's up to each of us to conduct ourselves without judgement and if curiosity strikes, to seek understanding that leads us all to a level of peace.

## SOCIAL PSYCHOLOGY OF MONADS AND EGREGORES

By technical terms a monad is formally defined as "a design pattern that allows structuring programs generically while automating away boilerplate code (codes with no alteration) needed by the *program logic*. Monads achieve this by providing their own data type, which represents a specific form of computation, along with one procedure to wrap values of any basic type within the monad (yielding a monadic value) and another to compose functions that output monadic values (called monadic functions)."- Wikipedia. This definition of monads also applies to the species in terms of soul groups. These soul groups break down from higher levels of consciousness into soul families and then into varying soulmate types. These relationships have been defined by many social psychologists including Plato.

An egregore is a thought form that belongs to a group level of consciousness. We have an egregore associated to everything we do, and an **egregore is what influences our thoughts, life choices, and actions**. We have one for all of our friends, family, communities, our careers, our spiritual beliefs, and most importantly... our level of consciousness. This consciousness is a soulless energy that are living thought forms tied to our auric fields. This is where the saying "you are what you attract" applies. The only difference in the perception is that the reality is that you could also be attracting what you need to heal from your programmed traumas not always that you attract exactly what you are. I was introduced and taught in depth about egrogores by healer and hypnotherapist Rose Siple of 'Thought Alchemy's Transformation Center' and continued my research and healing applications from there.

These egregores can also be manipulated by darkness and the more of us that feed into this energy field by exposing blockages or compound trauma patterns, these soulless egrogores can attract dark entities that will attach to these systems now creating entire monads operating under the will of this entity of darkness. This is why we see entire cities or some as widespread to countries and nations living in conditions plagued with too many misfortunes to name. Take a look at the trends in your relationships, your lifestyle, your community and careers...where do you stand? Are you engaging an egregore or darkness in some way? Have you escaped one? I most certainly have escaped more than one. Several as a matter of fact. Again, no judgement here because you don't know what you don't know until you do.

In order for us to help this planet or any monad we are a part of, we have to be conscious of these activities and band together to overpower them with light, wisdom, consciousness and love. That's the reason I'm doing what I'm doing. Even in the face of ridicule and the possibility of shame. And if you are in this space of judgement, ask yourself what led you there. And what lead you here. How do I know? Because I've done every single thing I've discussed within the contents of this material and then some. I've also been in the middle of these spectrums in my in-between stages of growth, clinging for dear life for those I didn't want to leave behind and ascend beyond. Slowly I realized I can't make anyone grow and some yield to the powers of darkness and don't even know.

# CHAPTER SIXTEEN
# CONCLUSION

## TREE OF LIFE AND METATRON'S CUBE

CONNECTING PATHS FROM 11 and 12 the sephira on the tree of life that correlates to the Sahasrara is the sephira Kether/Crown. This is the source of energy flow and powers the energy flow of the other 9 sephira's and resides at the top of our skull. The sephira 1 takes on a frequency that is indivisible but continues to project and clone itself in repetition in all that follows. Kether is the existence of beyond the human realm and within the hermetic principals is "The All in All." The is no physical form associated to the functions of this sephira, it is simply pure balanced energy. The God name for this sephira and level of consciousness is "Eheieh" which means existence. This is the purest level of existence and full balance of stoicism and full balance of the masculine and feminine within each of us.

The Arch Angel that oversees the functions of Kether is Arch Angel Metatron (who is one of my primary guides). Arch Angel Metatron is the only other angle other than Sandolphon to have been proven to have lived in human form, as Enoch, the grandfather of the biblical story of Noah and the author of the books of Enoch from the dead sea scrolls. While Enoch, Arch Angel Metatron gave us the most intact appendix to angelic beings, roles, and functions that we have access to within our societies today. His writings were removed from our modern-day bibles and can be found as quotes throughout varying quotes within the contexts of the Holy Bible, Quran, etc. that Christians, Jews, Muslims and many more spiritual context references today. The angelic order and realm associated to Kether is called Chaioth ha Qadesh meaning Holy Living Creatures.

Metatron oversees the flow of energy in soul conscious beings and is identified by the energetic shapes and flows of everything Elohim created. It contains every shape in the universe and is the most opulent form of sacred geometry. Metatron's cube represents how our souls ignite the energy within our bodies, and how they further unite with interstellar space. It is believed that this cube is what allows God's pure divine energy to flow into each of us when we are fully functioning and clear within our emotional bodies. At this point, we begin to activate the chakras, healing, and growth of other organisms. We can send and throw healthy electrical currents throughout time and space. At this point, we have reached full unity. Not just within unity consciousness but we begin the phase of unity with all that is, and we become the light of all there in a new light of consciousness of as above so below.

# METATRON CUBE

Years ago, by initiation of Arch Angel Metatron, also one of my guides, I was shown the purpose of my own souls' divinity. My entire purpose. I'd finally reached a space of superconscious thought through healing and was shown my lifespan not just in this incarnation, but from my soul's divinity. And I've seen many others for my clients at this point helping to heal the traumas of this life and the lives that have passed on in etheric imprint as coding in our DNA. It has become more and more apparent over time that my purpose is to illuminate truth based on the things I've seen and help the souls called to me to reach a new level of purification again. I have been doing this since the beginning of time.

For a long time in my life, my experiences bothered me but as a grew, I learned that because I was born into a bloodline that were both tied to some of the darkest egrogores and that I had a lot to do. And we can each do the work as we are called to. The other side of healing feels so good. I wouldn't change my experiences for a single thing if all I went through was to lead me to where I am today. I've been able to give my children a quantum leap in consciousness as a result. Something we can all do for generations to come.

I never understood why I was chosen for this call and why I was chosen to experience so much of what I thought was misfortune… I now realize that I was called to rise to the occasion in which I humbly accept. There is so much more to this… So much more, but for now, let's work as the call has been directed by spirit and I will now and will continue to offer all that I can. The curse/trauma associated to the Sahasrara is all that we have faced within our human experience. Everything that we experience that has kept us from the truth of our light as soul conscious beings…everything that has kept us in a deep state of oppression. Everything that has kept us from reaching our full potential… Everything that has kept us from being awake…But then… there was you. So, you woke up.

What do you need to know next? This was Metatron's instruction for right now. "Once you have read the full contents of this material and begun the steps necessary for your individual highest and best, the spell, root, episodic/generational curse, and attack will be broken. The necessary healing will open its way of life to you. This book is blessed. There will unfortunately be those that play out the experience of the 3rd dimensional reality and will not be ascending with us. Choosing to stay stuck in a traumatized state, or choosing dogma by rejecting ideals of unity consciousness, and as a result they will stay tied to this matrix grid reality as a result of fear. For them I pray for mercy. There is so much more than just this... but I hope for so many this is a healthy start.

How do you access the Metatron Cube state? This meditation will help: http://bit.ly/soiwokeup-cellular-enlightenment

Mother Earth is ascending to a new level of consciousness. Her cosmic name is Gaia she was created by the feminine aspect of Elohim whose name is Sophia. We owe it to Sophia to acknowledge her presence after such a long state of oppression deprived of her acknowledgment. We honor her by acknowledging and healing our emotional body. We owe it to Gaia, ourselves, and every species here sharing her space to heal traumas of the past and ascend with her to unity consciousness. "Have a blessed journey." It is my highest hope that this book, manual, and guide has helped YOU and began your awakening process.

Xoxo
Namaste,

Portia Dianne Lee
DBA Day Seven Wellness Center

# MY PERSONAL INVITATION TO YOU

Yes! You are about to go to your NEXT LEVEL! I know you have thoroughly enjoyed the book. I KNOW you are ready for change, but where does one begin? I am glad you asked. I have been working on this book for a long time and now that it is here, I WILL NOT leave halfway through your transformation.

I want to help you make the transition, from where you have been for far TOO long to where you have been wanting to go. This is why it is my honor to invite you to participate on the Trauma Release & Awakening Program.

In this amazing and powerful series of enlighten video sessions I will help you to... by the way, you can listen to this invitation here: http://bit.ly/trauma-release-program

**IN THE MEANTIME, HERE IS YOUR PERSONAL INVITATION:**

Hi, I'm Portia Dianne Lee, founder and CEO of Day Seven Wellness Center. Through Day Seven's Trauma Release and Awakening Program participants will unlock new levels of consciousness while further understanding the emotional body, allowing each participant to release store trauma from personal, social and environmental perspectives. As you've read in the book, so I woke up now what or will read, trauma does not have to be a personal or direct experience to have an impact on our lives.

This program will help each of us fully experience and identify traumas, signs, blockages and the physical effects that these traumas store within our emotional bodies. This program allows us to release the traumas using Day Seven Wellness Centers faith-based methods and guided meditation, affirmation, emotional freedom therapy, tapping, thought field therapy, and so much more.

This program introduces how social Psychology ties into the interaction we hold on a daily basis, and how they materialize within our relationships. This program provides strategies to empower our own emotional bodies and mental fitness to create and overcome our own personal triggers, as well as triggers for our loved ones and our peers.

Please join us to unlock the maximum potential of your wellness journey, allowing space to manifest the life of your dreams and holding a clear consciousness in space for your emotional body. Namaste!

Get ALL the information you need here:
http://bit.ly/trauma-release-program-details

# ABOUT THE AUTHOR

While the majority of us remain stagnant and complacent, the ever-evolving Portia D. Lee is constantly in pursuit of growth, healing, knowledge and ways to enhance and elevate her community. Portia is a loving mother of two boys and everything she does is for her children.

Portia is a natural born leader and has always excelled at whatever it is she has set her sights on. From being an excellent gymnast as a child to team captain of her national championship high school cheerleading team to being a business owner in her teens and early 20's. She has never been satisfied with just good enough or someone else trying to set her path.

Portia always knew there was something different about her and that there were certain gifts she possessed that she noticed her peers did not have. For example, Portia's first recollection of Astral travel was as a very young girl.

Portia's life journey and quest for enlightenment and ever-growing relationship with Spirit has made Portia very accomplished. Below is a list of her accolades:

- Master Reiki Practitioner
- Soul Master Practitioner
  Master Emotional Freedom Therapy and Thought Field Therapy EMT/TFT Practitioner
- Akashic Records Clairvoyant Reader and Healer

- Advanced Meditation
- Kinesiology
- Coaching & Training
- Yoga
- Psychology
- Cognitive Behavioral Therapy
- Harvard Extension Business School/ Strategic Management

Portia blends the perfect mixture of tenacity with patience which allows her to manage being a single mom, business owner, and always finding time for her community.

With the guidance of Spirit and fulfilling her own lifelong purpose, Portia aims to help as many people as possible to reach enlightenment, understanding, peace with self and facing and dealing with their own Personal Traumas.

Day Seven Wellness Center is Portia's vision of how to do just that. Taking her personal life mission and scaling it up to reach as many people as possible through Day Seven Wellness Center and Universal Achievers.

Another way Portia intends to help and touch as many people as possible is with the release of her first Published work "So I Woke Up... Now What." So, you can say, "So I Woke Up" has been a work in progress since Portia was a child. However, the knowledge, accolades, life experiences that Portia has garnered over the years and found in this book make this literary work extremely special, unique and life changing for the reader.

As eloquently written by Vare Raymond.

# REFERENCE PAGE

"The Power of God's Names" - Tony Evans

"The Book of Enoch"- Joseph B. Lumpkin

"Kabbalah for the Modern World"- Migene Gonzalez-Wippler

"Serpent of Light"- Drunvalo Melchizedek

"Autobiography of a Yogi"- Paramahansa Yogananda

"The Elegant Universe"- Brian Green

"Neurosis and Human Growth"- Karen Horney MD

"Sacred Geometry"- Stephen Skimmer

"The finding of Shambala"- James Redfield

"The finding of the Third Eye" / "The Fifth Dimension" - Vera Stanley Adler

Made in the USA
Las Vegas, NV
15 March 2022